發幾餘偶閱顧愷
史圀因寫幽蘭一
絹其窈窕相同之
云爾
青軒御識

## SYMBOLS, ART, AND LANGUAGE FROM THE LAND OF THE DRAGON

### THE CULTURAL HISTORY OF 100 CHINESE CHARACTERS

DUNCAN BAIRD PUBLISHERS

LONDON

## SYMBOLS, ART, AND LANGUAGE FROM THE LAND OF THE DRAGON

NI YIBIN

Distributed in the USA and Canada by
Sterling Publishing Co., Inc.
387 Park Avenue South
New York, NY 10016-8810

This edition first published in the UK and USA in 2009 by
Duncan Baird Publishers Ltd
Sixth Floor, Castle House
75–76 Wells Street
London W1T 3QH

ASSOCIATE AUTHOR: Peter Bently

MANAGING EDITOR: Kirty Topiwala
MANAGING DESIGNER: Manisha Patel
PICTURE RESEARCH: Julia Ruxton
COMMISSIONED ARTWORK: Yukki Yaura

Library of Congress Cataloging-in-Publication Data

Ni, Yibin.
  Symbols, art, and language from the land of the dragon : the cultural history of
100 Chinese characters / Ni Yibin.
     p. cm.
  Includes bibliographical references and index.
  ISBN 978-1-84483-849-3
  1.  Chinese characters--History.  I. Title.
  PL1171.N6 2009
  495.1'11--dc22
                              2009012691

ISBN: 978-1-84483-849-3

10 9 8 7 6 5 4 3 2 1

Typeset in DIN
Color reproduction by Scanhouse
Printed in China by Imago

For information about custom editions, special sales, premium and corporate
purchases, please contact Sterling Special Sales Department at 800-805-5489 or
specialsales@sterlingpub.com.

**NOTES:**
Abbreviations used throughout this book:
CE Common Era (the equivalent of AD)
BCE Before the Common Era (the equivalent of BC)

**FRONT AND BACK ENDPAPERS:** Sections of a handscroll illustrating the
*Nushi zen* (Admonitions of the Instructress of the Ladies in the Palace),
by Zhuang Hua (ca. 232–300CE), with seals and colophons from the
Huizong and Qianlong emperors.

**PAGE 4:** Hanging scroll in cursive script by Deng Shiru (1743–1805).

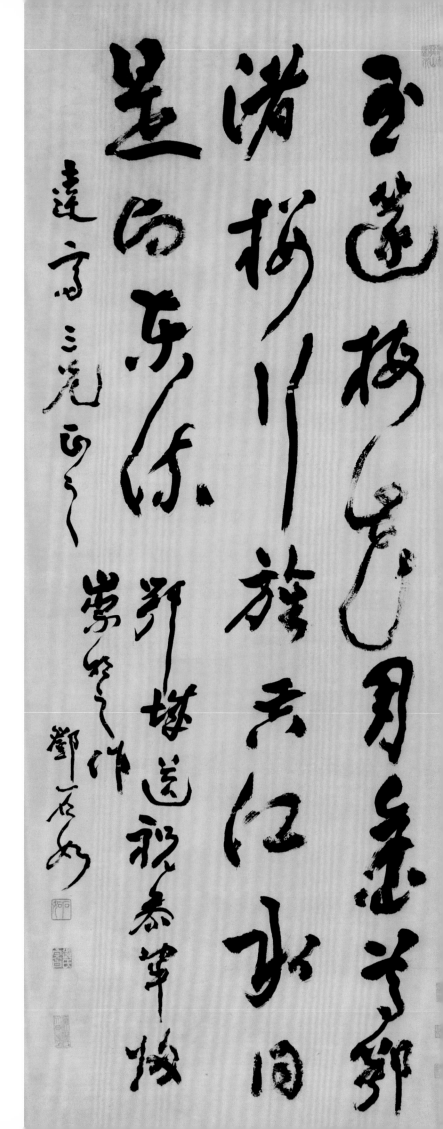

# CONTENTS

# Introduction

**ABOVE: Text inscribed onto a bronze bell dating from the Western Zhou dynasty (ca. 1046–770BCE). This type of script is known as "bronze script", which succeeded the more rigid "oracle bone script" that developed in the Shang dynasty, around the 11th–12th centuries BCE.**

Chinese characters are the written or printed forms of words in the Chinese language. They are significant because they belong to one of the very few writing systems still in use today that have a long and unbroken evolutionary history. What's more, owing to the currently huge number of ethnic Chinese, these characters will continue to be used by more people than any other written language in the world.

Unlike most languages, Chinese is non-alphabetical. In an alphabetical language, the basic elements in a written word are selected from a limited set of letters – an alphabet. The arrangement of these letters shows the reader how the word should be pronounced, but each individual letter has no meaning of its own. By contrast, a Chinese character is composed of one or more "root characters" (radicals), selected from a set of more than 400, which usually have a meaning as well as an associated pronunciation. Most early Chinese words had just one syllable and were thus represented by only one of these characters. In modern times, however, a Chinese spoken word usually consists of more than one syllable, and is put down on paper in the form of one, two or more characters accordingly. Unlike words that consist of meaningless letters from an alphabet, each resulting character has a meaning component or a sound component, or both. There are seemingly endless permutations – the latest official coded character set that is used on computers to type Chinese characters (called "GB18030") can encode as many as 27,533 characters, although only 3,000 of these characters are actually needed to read 99 per cent of Chinese texts.

The unique complexity and symbolism of these character forms, and the ways in which they have been expressed through varying scripts and styles, lie at the heart of Chinese culture and history.

## Ancient Beginnings

According to Chinese mythology, the creator of writing was a legendary historian called Cang Jie. He is supposed to have invented a series of basic characters relating to the particular characteristics that distinguish different natural forms from one another, such as paw and hoof prints, or grass and trees. It is said that the birth of Chinese characters was so important for the world that nature acknowledged their creation with mysterious miracles, like showers of grain and the howling of demons.

In reality, the earliest forms of character-like forms occurred in China around 8,000 years ago, and a mature writing system was in use by the late Shang dynasty, around the 11th–12th centuries BCE. Many examples of these early rune-like characters have been found inscribed on ox shoulder-blade bones or tortoise shells. They were written there in order to communicate with ancestors who were thought to be able to protect their descendants' interests from the afterlife, and this form of writing is therefore known as "oracle bone script".

Characters were also written on bamboo slats or tablets with brushes at this time, as implied by the discovery of an inscribed character meaning "texts written on bamboo slips". Because they were arranged in vertical columns, some characters were rotated 90 degrees in order to fit the narrow constraints of bamboo slats, a feature that transferred to other writing surfaces as well, and explains the vertical appearance of oracle bone characters such as that for "tortoise" (gui, see figure 2).

Unfortunately these more perishable materials have not survived, and oracle bone examples are, therefore, the earliest extant texts available today. Carved into a hard and slippery surface using sharp metal tools, the oracle bone script is characterized by straight lines of the same width, with very few round turns. At this stage, the characters were also by no means uniform, and there were often improvised strokes for the same character on different occasions.

Characters dating from the dynasty that followed the Shang, the Zhou (ca. 1046–221BCE), have been found on ritual bronze vessels, and are therefore known as "bronze script". These texts often describe the political events and social relationships central to the lives of the Zhou élite. The characters were generally inscribed onto a clay mould, from which the entire vessel was later cast. Curved lines and complex forms could be much more easily carved into wet clay than directly onto a hard surface as the oracle bone script was. As a result there are more round turns, more intricate designs and greater consistency in forms of the same character in the bronze script.

Both the oracle bone and bronze scripts are regarded as "epigraphic" scripts. Most of the one hundred characters discussed in this book have their four main development stages illustrated alongside them on the page, beginning with the epigraphic stage, in order to demonstrate their pictographic origin and the possible rationale behind their evolution. The epigraphic forms of about ten per cent of the characters chosen are still undiscovered, however, and are shown with just the three later development stages – the seal, clerical and standard scripts.

**Styles of written communication: the establishment of the earliest characters**

In ancient times, the simplest way to create a character was to draw a sketch of the thing to be represented, such as that for "moon"

1: One of the earliest graphs for the character 月 *yue* for "moon".

2: One of the earliest graphs for the character 龜 *gui* meaning "tortoise".

3: The character 采 *cai* meaning "to pick" or "to gather" was originally created by combining the pictures of a hand (*above*) and a plant (*below*).

(*yue, see figure 1*) or for "tortoise" (*gui, see figure 2*). In order for these early pictures or "pictographs" to become proper written words, ie characters, they had to be repeatedly related to a corresponding spoken word in the language. That is, every proper character – for example, that for "tortoise" (*gui*) – had to have three basic aspects: its distinctive form (its early epigraphic form, *figure 2*, or later forms, including the present-day 龜), its pronunciation (*gui*) and its meaning (the animal, tortoise). Although limited, this method, which creates simple, non-composite characters, was very useful at the early stages in the development of the Chinese writing system. Most of these non-composite characters also appeared later as part of composite characters.

When an action rather than an object was to be represented, a combined ("composite") picture was often created to form the character. For example, the earliest character for the word *cai*, meaning the action "to pick/gather (food from plants)", shows a plant or tree with a hand above it (*see figure 3*), in order to illustrate this meaning. The lower element is a character in its own right when it appears alone, originally meaning "plant" but today meaning "wood" (*mu*). Most existing Chinese characters are composite characters in the manner of *cai*.

More ways of representing the world pictorially were still needed and in turn invented, often by adapting existing characters. For example, the concept of a "knife edge" (*ren*) was indicated, rather than illustrated, by adding a line to the edge of the pictographic character for "knife" (*dao, see figure 4*).

In this way, therefore, characters were invented for those objects, people, actions and relationships that can be directly portrayed.

**4:** The main element in the composite character for "knife edge" (刃 *ren*) is the non-composite character for "knife" (刀 *dao*). A line was added to its epigraphic form (*left*) to indicate the edge of the knife (*right*). This line later evolved into a dot in the current-day 刃 *ren* character.

**5:** The character 又 *you* originally created for "right hand", shown here in its epigraphic (*left*) and standard (*right*) forms, was later used to denote the concept of "also" because the pronunciation of the two Chinese words was similar.

**6:** The top-radical of "plants" was added to the epigraphic form of the character 采 *cai* for "to pick" or "to gather" (*left*) to create the character 菜 *cai* for "vegetable" (*right*).

**7:** The epigraphic forms of the character 魚 *yu* for "fish" (*left*) and the character 白 *bai* for "white" (*right*).

**8:** The seal script (*left*) and standard script (*right*) forms of the character 鮊 *bo* for "*bo* fish".

However, other means were required in order to cater for more complicated linguistic cases – after all, not everything in the world can be literally represented by a simple picture. One way to denote a word that cannot easily be represented by a pictograph is to "borrow" another character that has the same spoken pronunciation to do the job. To give an example, the Chinese word for "also", pronounced *you*, sounds similar to the word for "right", also pronounced *you*. The character for "right", which was originally created to represent "right hand", was therefore used to denote "also" as well (*see figure 5*). This "borrowing" of characters for their sound value in written word creation, also known as the "rebus" use of pictographs, is very common in linguistic development and is found in many ancient civilizations such as Egypt, Mesopotamia and Maya.

Interestingly, after an existing character had been borrowed and invested with different meaning, a new character was then sometimes created to exclusively represent the meaning of the original character. This meant that the borrowed character could denote its new meaning unambiguously. For example, originally, the character 云 *yun* denoted "cloud". Later, *yun* (云) was borrowed to denote the verb "said". Soon afterwards, a new character for cloud was formed (雲), incorporating a *yu* radical (雨) for "rain" on top of the original *yun* (云) because of the close association between cloud and rain. From then on this new character (雲) exclusively denoted "cloud", leaving the original, borrowed *yun* (云) exclusively for the function of the verb "said". (*See also* CLOUD, *p22.*)

When, again, these ways of creating characters proved insufficient to represent the spoken language used in early China, a revolutionary new way was introduced. This new method was based on the same principle of "sound-element borrowing" discussed above, with an existing character being used as the pronunciation element in a new character. However, another element was also added to indicate the *meaning* of the new character. This proved to be the simplest and most efficient method for creating characters to match the vast and ever-expanding vocabulary of Chinese speech. For example, the character denoting "vegetable", pronounced *cai*, was created by adding a top-radical meaning "grass" to an existing character, discussed on page 7, which is also pronounced *cai* but means "to pick/gather" (*see figure 6*). Characters created in this way are, therefore, often the homophone or near-homophone of another character – in this case the character for "to pick/gather" is the homophone of the character for "vegetable".

This type of character is composed of two basic parts: one that indicates how it is pronounced and one that signifies the meaning of the character. In the case of *cai* ("vegetable"), the lower part, the original

9: The general development of the character 犬 *quan* for "dog", through various stages of oracle bone and bronze scripts. The last two characters are in seal and clerical scripts respectively.

character for the verb "to pick/gather", functions as the pronunciation element and provides a clue as to how the new character should sound, while the upper part, the top-radical that looks like two plants, reveals that the new character has something to do with plants.

The efficiency of this method can also be demonstrated by the series of characters that were invented for varieties of fish. Each different variety was represented by a radical that shares a similar sound to its name, but was also accompanied by a "fish" radical to make the context clear. For example, the character for a type of fish called *bo* combines the radical for "white" (today pronounced *bai,* but originally said more like *bo*), to indicate the pronunciation and the radical for "fish", to show that it is a fish (*see figures 7 and 8*). This method was also used for other "varieties" within a species or group, such as types of vegetable.

The bulk of modern-day characters were formed by this last method, which should in theory make them easier to decipher. However, the original pronunciation of many characters has naturally changed over time, so today many of them are no longer pronounced in the manner intended at their creation. This factor incidentally adds a burden to students of the Chinese language, because they often need to learn the correct pronunciation of characters one by one, instead of simply following the pronunciation element present in each character.

**Diversification and standardization: the further development of characters in the Qin and Han dynasties**

In general, as these characters became more widely circulated, they also became less pictographic and more stylized and standardized for convenience of use (*see figure 9*).

After the First Emperor, Qin Shi Huangdi (259–210BCE) of the Qin dynasty, achieved national unification in China in 221BCE, he ensured that the Chinese script was also unified for efficient written communication across the vast landmass and diversified communities of the new empire. Previously, different principalities had used their own epigraphic scripts, which have been discovered on excavated bronze vessels, bamboo and wooden slips, and silk sheets. Many of these scripts consisted of pictographs of different sizes, as well as improvised pictorial elements.

The new official script, called *xiao-zhuan*, was based on a script already used in the Qin state, and standardized the different regional forms into stylized characters written in regular, vertically oblong shapes, and in even, macaroni-like lines. Well-defined spacing between neighbouring characters and columns also made the script easier to read.

The process of standardizing diversified characters was carried out together with the standardization of other social institutions, such as weights and measures, currency and legal statutes. As a result, *xiao-zhuan* became the dominant script throughout China by law and, therefore, the ancestor of all the later Chinese character scripts. A series of texts in this script still exist in China, carved on stones, eulogizing the First Emperor's great achievements. The Chinese word *zhuan* literally means "writing with a brush", and the reason the emperor named this script *xiao-zhuan* was that he intended it to be *the* Chinese script. It is known more specifically as *xiao-zhuan* ("lesser" *zhuan*) is to distinguish it from *da-zhuan* ("greater" *zhuan*), a name that was reserved for the more pictorial variety of bronze writing popular during the Shang and Zhou dynasties. After the Han dynasty, when the clerical script became more widely used, *xiao-zhuan* was mainly employed on stamping-seals, because its beauty lends itself well to the constraints of a seal's composition. From then on it also became known as "seal script". Most Chinese people are not able to read the seal script today. However, it is still often used by calligraphers in order to enhance the sense of antiquity evoked by a text or decorated object, or to display his or her virtuosity as a calligrapher.

In addition to the official and more formal "seal script", a more practical script appeared around the Qin and Han dynasties, known as the "clerical script" (*see figure 10*). It gained the title "clerical", or, in Chinese, *li-shu* (literally, "the writing of petty officials"), because of its popularity among government clerks. Appearing as horizontally rectangular characters, clerical script was even more simplified in form, and thus more convenient to use, than the seal script. Between the 3rd century BCE and the 2nd century CE, it developed rapidly and was widely seen on wooden and bamboo slips for texts ranging from military reports to sex manuals. In the Han dynasty (206BCE–220CE), the

**10: Comparison of the seal script (*left*) and the clerical script (*right*) forms of the character 龍 *long* meaning "*long* dragon".**

clerical script experienced a major reform and became more regular, abstract and distinctively symbol-like. This post-reform version of clerical script marked the most important milestone in the history of Chinese characters because it was the point of departure from their pictographic stage. Han clerical script also started to incorporate calligraphic features, such as the varying thickness and slight flourish of the horizontal lines, that give away the movement of the feathery brush tip. It was these features that previous scripts had lacked and the later calligraphic arts would treasure. The Han form is still the standard version of the clerical script that Chinese calligraphers use today.

### The art of writing: the beginnings of calligraphy

The Chinese word *shu-fa* loosely translates as "calligraphy" in English. However, this term means something very different to Chinese people than it does to Westerners. When the Greeks coined the term *kalligraphia*, meaning "beautiful writing", they were a people who used an alphabetical writing, just like the modern English, German and French. So what they meant by "calligraphy" was something like a painstaking, stylized, prettified writing. However, for the Chinese, *shu-fa* (literally "method of writing") or *shu-dao* ("way of writing") is the most revered of all art forms, above those that are regarded as "high art" in the West such as painting, sculpture and architecture. Chinese calligraphy can be compared to Abstract Expressionism and "action painting", as represented by Jackson Pollock's "drip" technique, in that what the calligrapher leaves on the paper is not just the literal meaning of the text communicated by the characters, but also traces of movement, speed and force. Furthermore, for Chinese scholars or *literati* throughout the ages, practising calligraphy is an act of divination and an expression of the calligrapher's sensibility and psychic powers.

There is a material basis for the differences in the Western and Chinese view of calligraphy. Firstly, as already mentioned, the Chinese script is non-alphabetical and has tens of thousands of different character combinations to choose from. And not only is the repertoire of forms much larger than that of the mere dozens of letters in any known

Western alphabet, but the characters themselves are far more diverse and complex than letters. Secondly, the Chinese brush-pen (*see also* PEN, *p144*) is crucially different from the Western hard, pointed pen. A Western pen – even the earliest quill or stylus – leaves far more regular, less varied traces of ink than those left by a Chinese brush-pen, whose conic, soft and flexible tip records the calligrapher's every minute movement and pause like a seismograph.

As early as the Bronze Age in China, engraved inscriptions on ceremonial bronze vessels began to be less perfunctory and more decorative. In fact, skillful craftsmen were being employed to adorn these vessels with calligraphic texts in order to convey the dignity and status of their owners. However, it was not until around the late 2nd and early 3rd centuries, that a significant double shift took place in the history of Chinese calligraphy: anonymous craftsmen became venerated calligraphers, and the purpose of this "beautiful writing" changed from being simple embellishment to a manifestation of the artist's inner self.

### The emergence of the final three scripts

This period also coincided with the emergence of the remaining three important Chinese scripts: the *kai* standard script, the *xing* running script and the *cao* cursive script.

The origins of the *kai-shu* or *zhen-shu* ("standard script") can be traced back to the Han dynasty, when it began as a further regulation of the clerical script. Unlike clerical script, which has sweeping strokes with accented beginnings and dramatically pointed ends, and unlike seal script, which has rounded corners and organic forms, the short, bland strokes and basic, terse structure of standard script make it even easier to recognize and write. Within each character of the standard script, thick and slender strokes alternate rhythmically and turns and hooks are distinctively articulated – in combination they convey a sense of discipline and constrained energy. By the 3rd century the standard script was already being widely used and it has remained the most

**RIGHT: Composition of four characters in large seal script by the master calligrapher Li Ruiqing (1876–1920), mounted on a larger sheet displaying five texts in clerical script (*uppermost*) and running script (*others*), respectively attributed to Zeng Xi, Zhang Daqian, Li Ruiqi, Li Jian and Hu Xianshi. These surrounding texts praise Li Ruiqing and describe how the four central characters were obtained by his student Zhang Daqian.**

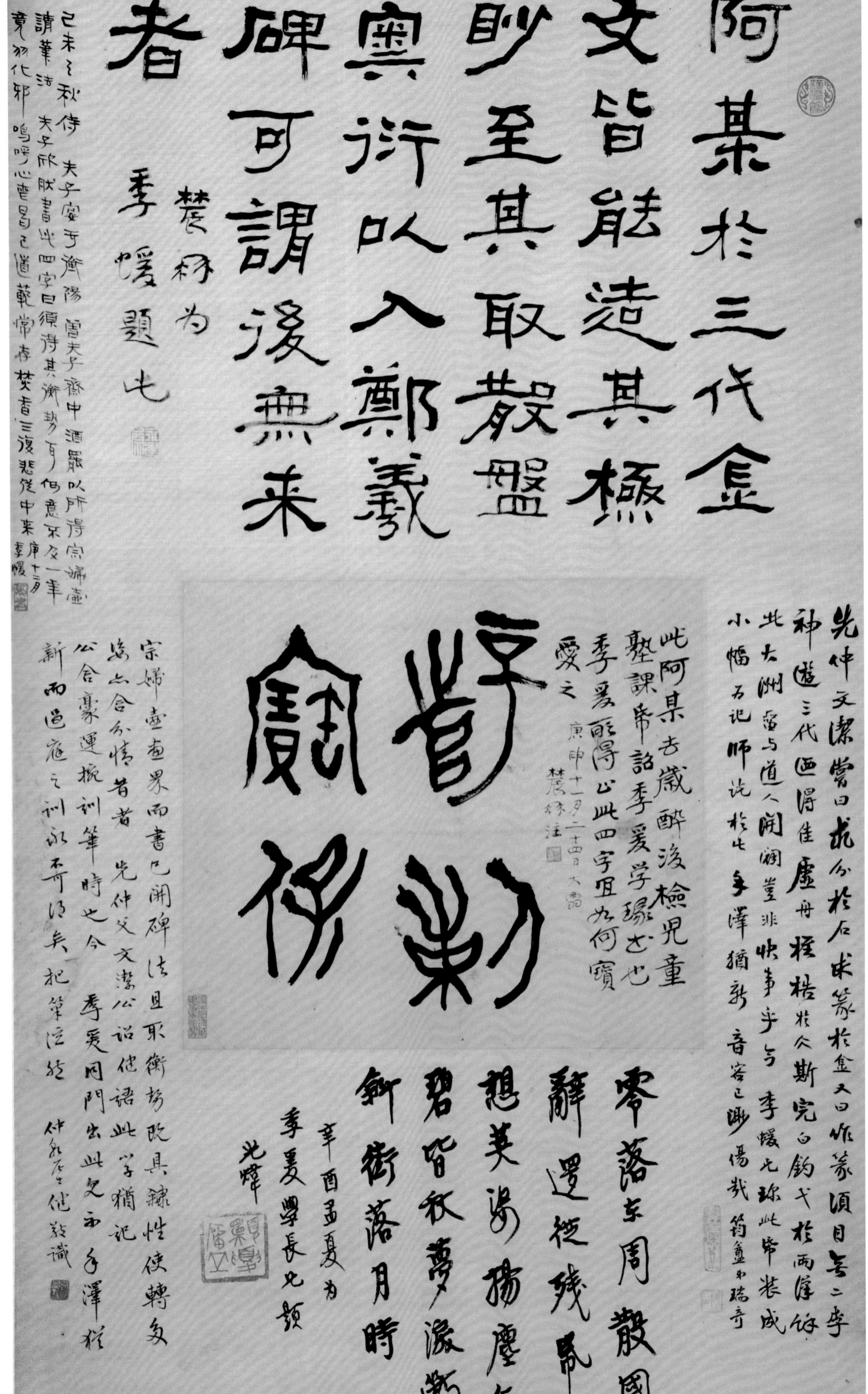

阿某於三代金

文皆骸遠其橅

眇至其取榖盤

寅術以入鄭義

碑可謂後無來

者

裝籵為

季媛題七

此阿某去歲醉後檢兒童
塾課帋詬季愛學璩古也
季愛輙得此此四字丑九何寶
愛之
庚申十二月二十四日大寒
麓綠注

先仲文潔嘗曰龈分於栖石求篆於金又曰作篆須目寄二季
神遊三代迴得佳處舟程格狀公斯完西鈞弋扵兩淖好
北大洲磊与道人開潤崟非快事乎与李媛先琢此帋峩成
小幀石記師詫扵七手澤猶新音容之邈陽我筠篁中瑞尋

零落東周散國
辭還他綫鼠
君皆秋夢激渺街
新衢落月時之
光輝
辛酉孟夏為
季愛學長七頊

此阿某去歲醉後檢兒童

宗婦遠壺罨而書已開碑法且耴衡枋歐具辣性使轉多
臨六合分情昔者 先仲文文潔公詒他語此學猶記
公合豪運振訓筆時之今 季愛同門出此文而子澤程
新西迴庀完利邴奇為兵耙筆法終
仲郎虚他敬識

己未之秋侍 夫子宴于潯陽 官夫子齋中酒罷以所得宗婦壺
請華注 夫子欣書此四字曰纘得其衡勢且何意京及一軍
竟物化邨鳴呼心管昌之道蕐常春焚香三復悲從中來季媛
陽書

popular style of writing the Chinese language to this day. It is also the form adopted for the printed Chinese script. Standard script is classified in three varieties according to size: large (*da-kai*), medium (*zhong-kai*) and small (*xiao-kai*), and it is said that the disciplined calligrapher should regard the hips as the axis of brush movement when writing *da-kai*, the shoulder when writing *zhong-kai*, and the elbow when writing *xiao-kai*.

Developed in the 2nd century CE, the *xing-shu*, or "running script", is an everyday-writing version of the *kai-shu* standard script, with greater freedom of strokes. Popular for less formal modes of communication, such as personal correspondence and inscriptions on Chinese paintings, it can be written quickly, but retains legibility. What is arguably the most famous piece of calligraphy in Chinese history, *Langting Ji Xu* (*Preface to the Orchid Pavilion Collection*), was written in running script by Wang Xizhi (303–361CE), the so-called "sacred calligrapher" of China.

The *cao-shu* "cursive script" is freer still in brushstroke than running script, and therefore not as easy to read. It was originally a shorthand version of the clerical and standard scripts, enabling characters to be written more quickly and with greater freedom, by abbreviating forms, combining strokes and omitting sections of radicals. Because of its loose and expressive character, *cao shu* was considered a particularly beautiful script, with a beauty that many believe reached its peak with

the skill of Tang Buddhist monk Huaisu (active ca. 730–780CE), who wrote in an extreme version of the script known as "wild cursive" (*kuang-cao*). With its own stroke sequence and somewhat conventionalized forms,

**TOP RIGHT:** Album leaf by the calligrapher Bada Shenren (1626–1705), transcribing in running script a poem entitled *On Stopping for the Evening at Deer Gate Mountain* by the Tang-dynasty poet Yan Fang.

**BELOW LEFT:** Woodcut print from *A Manual of Calligraphy and Painting from the Ten Bamboo Studio* by Hu Zhengyan (ca. 1582–ca. 1672). The standard script text on the left-hand side is a poem by He Shikun of Guangzhou about plum blossom.

**BELOW RIGHT:** Section from the autobiography of the Tang dynasty Buddhist monk Huaisu, famed for his use of wild cursive script. This piece dates from 777CE.

**FOLLOWING PAGES:** Painting of an orchid (ca. 1692), with an inscription in cursive script praising the delicacy and fragrance of the flower, probably executed by a Chinese monk of the Obaku sect of Zen Buddhism.

龐公嘉遁所 浪迹難追攀浮舟
瞑怡岂扼扶弥自甫渡奎間鹿門百
谷集珠灣噴薄滿上水舂容臬襄
山樵原丑險峻果峯未威難我行目
仲春夏島语絲窒畺料名之晚窗心
谷来還遠游州囘地訪迄受童颜
安能狥揆巧争奪錐刀间
順非正人書
笑人

時壬申之初秋
琅西阿偶寫

風散芳蓮都
花清白露重

*kuang-cao* would only have been easily decipherable by those closest to the calligrapher, and therefore conveys a sense of intimacy among friends. What's more, the infinite variation in the shape and thickness of the strokes, the gradations of tone and the proportion of black ink to white paper, all at the calligrapher's disposal, have made wild cursive script an ideal form to express one's spontaneity. Another *kuang-cao* master, Zhang Xu (active 713–740CE), took his inspiration from the rhythm, postures and movements of sword dancing, one of the ancient martial arts in China. The brushstrokes in this script's style, as described by a 3rd-century calligrapher and theorist, "can be as smooth as a silver hook, or light as a startled bird, with wings outspread but not yet flying, as if lifting, then settling back". Often inspired by drinking wine, *kuang-cao* is characterized by very rapid and fleeting touches of the brush-tip, and is appreciated for its direct externalization of powerful psychic states.

It was, in fact, the economy of strokes and simplicity of forms employed in these cursive scripts that formed the basis for the modern "simplified" set of Chinese characters. While the simplified character set shares many identical forms with the "traditional" set, many of the more complex characters have been reduced to more basic and essential forms. Simplified characters are in wide use today in China; however, traditional characters are still used in Taiwan, Hong Kong, Macau and many overseas Chinese communities. In this book all of the characters are traditional, except for those in the Chinese text of the proverbs and sayings, which include some simplified forms.

### An expression of the true self: calligraphy flourishing

In pursuing the spiritual and formal beauty of writing, the *literati* of the Six Dynasties (220–589CE), from the fall of the Han dynasty to the beginning of the Sui dynasty, cultivated calligraphy as a mark of their distinction. Ever since then, it has been the *way* that calligraphy texts are written, rather than their meaning, that has been revered and admired, and this is reflected in the way that calligraphy collections are traditionally categorized – according to type of script (such as *cao-shu*, *kai-shu* or *xing-shu*), rather than their literary contents (such as poetry, letters or essays).

The special arrangement of brushstrokes in a piece of calligraphy can often help to express the content of the text, but, more importantly, should be considered a reflection of the emotions, personality and creativity of their writer. For example, Sun Guoting's *Shu Pu* (*Manual of Calligraphy*) of 648CE describes how the happiness and wine-fuelled thoughts of calligrapher Wang Xizhi, when writing about the meeting of 42 *literati* friends at the Orchid Pavilion in the famous *Langting Ji Xu* (*Preface to the Orchid Pavilion Collection*), are expressed by his choice of "untrammelled strokes". A master calligrapher can vary the touch, speed and movement of the brush to produce the lightest or boldest of strokes in countless combinations, as though performing an acrobatic feat. He or she commands and manipulates the tools and materials to create the perfect contrast of black ink and white paper, light and shadow, energy and calm. The process of writing can, therefore, be considered a form of early performance art, and a connoisseur should be able to reconstruct this performance from a finished piece of calligraphy, empathizing with the mood and intention of the master, and appreciating their skill and creativity. The Northern Song calligrapher Mi Fu (1052–1107) expressed his love of calligraphy in the following words: "Every time I spread out a scroll, I am oblivious even to the roar of thunder by my side, and the taste of food is forgotten ... I suspect that after I die I will become a silverfish who enters into scrolls."

Despite the great potential for freedom of expression, a calligrapher is still constrained by certain conventions – from how to hold and use the brush to the particular sequence that must be followed to form a character. He or she must have full command of the Four Treasures of the Scholar's Study – brushes, paper, ink and ink stone – and be able to follow the vertically linear structure of Chinese writing columns, which read from top to bottom, left to right (a convention that probably resulted from writing on strips of bamboo and wood). What's more, they must be able to choose the style and script-type appropriate to the content and purpose of the text they are writing. A calligrapher has to train rigorously for years, even for an entire lifetime, in order to manoeuvre comfortably within these constraints. Ultimately, each act of writing is a struggle between age-old tradition and the calligrapher's creative spirit. A champion calligrapher will accept the challenge, and make the most of this great opportunity to express his or her true self.

**RIGHT: An elderly calligrapher writes down his customer's wishes for the forthcoming year in the run-up to Chinese New Year.**

**FAR RIGHT: Calligraphy brushes are organized into types according to different animal hairs, which provide each one with a unique texture and stroke.**

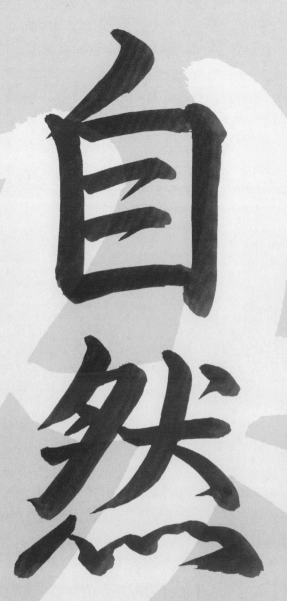

自然

NATURE

天 地 雲 星 日
月 春 夏 秋 冬
山 田 川 海 水
火 木 土 石 龍
鳳 鶴 鹿 龜 魚
牛 馬 犬 象 松
竹 蓮 梅 桂

# HEAVEN

## TIAN

天道亏盈而益谦

**"The Way of Heaven is to make the full wane and the scanty increase."**

In its epigraphic stage, 天 *tian* originally meant "top of the head" and was therefore shaped like a person with a large head. It then came to denote "sky" because the sky was the only thing that existed naturally above the top of a primitive man's head when he stood in the fields. In its contemporary form, *tian* has lost its large head, and instead a horizontal bar is placed on top of the character *da*, which resembles a human shape with stretched arms and legs and means "large".

Since the sky was such an awesome phenomenon, *tian* was used by people in the Zhou dynasty (ca. 1046–221BCE) as a name for their highest god. The cult of the divinity "Tian" flourished during the Zhou dynasty and from then

on the word came to be synonymous with the idea of Heaven and the cosmos.

China's early kings also adopted the title *tian*, to glorify the concept of their supernatural power over their subjects and land (*see also* KING, *p92*). This association between Heaven and the imperial power justified a king's mandate – his right to wield absolute political and religious power. The title "Son of Heaven" was inherited by all the emperors throughout dynastic China. Later, Christian missionaries made use of this indigenous idea and translated the name for their Christian God into Chinese as *tian zhu* – "Master of Heaven".

Since the concept of Heaven played such an important role in social and political life, people were put "in charge" of observing *tian* in ancient China. Oracle bone inscriptions record eclipses and novae in the second millennium BCE, while detailed observations of the sky were recorded from the 6th century BCE, long before the arrival of the Western telescope at the Chinese court in the 16th century.

The word *tian* can also denote "day", "weather" or "season", so "today" is *jin tian* (*jin* means "this moment") and a "good *tian*" is a "fine day".

# EARTH
**DI**

天地不合，万物不生
**"If Heaven and Earth are not in harmony, nothing on Earth will be healthy."**

To the ancient Chinese, the Earth seemed to be basically made of soil, and so the character for "Earth" 地 *di*, developed with a 土 *tu* radical that denotes "soil" at its left. The element at the right-hand side is believed to represent either the female reproductive organs or a vessel, and originally functioned as a pronunciation indicator.

According to the early Chinese philosophical ideas of *yin* and *yang* (*see pp152–153*), everything in the universe has a counterpart. The counterpart of the dome-like round Heaven (*see opposite*) is the Earth, which they believed to be square, lying beneath it. The combination of the two words, *tian di* – "Heaven and Earth", denotes the whole universe. According to the ancient Chinese world view, the universe started as the egg of chaos. In time, Heaven and Earth split open: the *yang*, which was light and clear, became Heaven, and the *yin*, which was heavy and murky, became Earth. Unlike the Judeo-Christian tradition in the West, China did not have creation myths involving an almighty creator. Instead, supernatural beings took part only in transforming an earlier world into a new one. One popular version from southern China tells how the various features on Earth began as parts of a creature named Pan Gu, who grew larger and larger as Heaven rose higher and higher and Earth became thicker and thicker. His four limbs and torso became the four poles and the central point in between them, and also the Five Great Mountains of China; his blood turned into rivers; his sinews and muscle into geographic features and soil; and his skin-hairs into grasses and trees.

In Chinese culture, the four poles and their centre point are each associated with different colours, planets, seasons, natural elements, sacred animals and so on. This forms the basis of correlative cosmology – a theory that tried to explain the workings of the universe and to legitimate imperial power.

# CLOUD

**YUN**

不义而富且贵，于我如浮云
*Confucius said,* **"Riches and prestige gained through dishonourable means are to me as fleeting clouds."**

The epigraphic character for 雲 *yun*, meaning "cloud", is an image of swirling cloud vapour. Because the Chinese word for "to say" was also pronounced *yun*, the character for "cloud" was originally used to denote both meanings. Later, the radical for "rain" (雨) was added on top to create a new character to specifically denote "cloud", and this forms the basis for the present-day traditional character (雲). However, *yun* meaning "to say" is now antiquated, and users

of the modern simplified script have reverted to the original character for cloud (云).

Formed, according to Chinese myth, from the breath of the cosmic giant Pan Gu (*see* EARTH, *p21),* clouds are denizens of the celestial realm and bringers of nourishing rain. As such they are considered auspicious symbols, particularly when they contain colours.

Clouds have an additional important symbolic association. The earliest account of the

Chinese notion of the human soul, dating from the 6th century BCE, states that life begins in the womb with the "moon-soul" (*po*). Then, on taking its first breath of air (*qi*) at birth, a baby is also infused with what is known as a "cloud-soul" (*hun*), which originates in the heavens. If properly nurtured, it is believed that these two souls will become strong and even attain "spiritual brightness", a term which is connected to the much-desired state of immortality. Indeed, in

later Chinese tradition, immortals are sometimes described as residing in palaces in the clouds.

While the *po* remained with the body after death, it was thought that the *hun* floated away, returning to the heavens. To prevent any potential trouble from the *hun*, the relatives of the deceased might try to encourage it to return to the body through rituals and offerings. (*See also* SOUL, *p80.*)

雲

雲
雲
雲

BELOW: Low clouds at dawn over
the Huangshan mountains in Anhui
province, eastern China.

# STAR

## XING

井中视星，所见不过数星

**"If one observes stars from inside a well, one may mistakenly believe that there are only a few stars in the sky."**

Constellations were regarded in ancient China as the essence of all things on Earth, elevated to the sky and hung like pearls under the canopy of the heavens. To represent this connection between the earthly and the celestial, early forms of the character 星 *xing* represent heavenly bodies seen among the branches of a tree; in some later forms (not shown here), they were shown dangling from branches. In the seal script form of the character, the constellations were reduced to the 日 *ri* character, meaning "sun", above the tree image simplified to the character 生 *sheng*.

As recorded more than 3,000 years ago, the Chinese classified the stars into 28 constellations, thought to correspond with the administrative areas on Earth – an idea that became the basis for their holistic view of the world. By the 2nd century BCE, 11,520 stars had been counted and recorded in China.

Among them, two of the most famous are the "Cowherd" and the "Weaving Maid", known in the West today as Altair and Vega respectively. Both are high and prominent in the night sky in late summer, and were therefore associated with a romantic Chinese legend. One day, a young cowherd came across seven fairies bathing in a lake, having left their clothes unguarded. Mischievously, he took away the most beautiful of the sets of clothes and hid himself to see what would happen. It turned out that the clothes he had taken belonged to the seventh sister, who was skilled at making fabrics, and known as the weaving maid. The other six fairies put on their clothes and flew back to Heaven, leaving their youngest sister behind, reluctant to return naked. The cowherd and the weaving maid then fell in love and bore two children. However, the goddess of Heaven was furious to discover that a mortal had married her daughter, and forced the weaving maid to come home. With the help of his ox, the cowherd managed to catch up with the weaving maid on her journey back, but the goddess of Heaven then used her hair-pin to scratch a line in the sky to separate the two lovers. This scratch is said to have become the Milky Way, which still keeps the couple apart today, except for one day of the year – the seventh day of the seventh month. On this day, when the stars are particularly visible and the weather is generally good, magpies are supposed to form a bridge across the Milky Way to reunite the lovers for just one night.

日月如梭

**"The coming and going of the sun and the moon
is as fast as a shuttle on a loom."**

# SUN
## RI

The character 日 *ri* for "sun" evolved from earlier rounded forms that resemble the spherical heavenly body. According to the oldest dictionary in China, the *Shuo-wen jie-zi* (*Explanations of Simple Graphs and Analyses of Composite Graphs*, compiled by Xu Shen and presented at court in 121CE), the black dot in the centre of the circle indicates that the sun is full of the essence of the masculine *yang* force in nature (*see p153*). Hence, the colloquial Chinese name for the sun is *tai yang*, "the supreme *yang*". As the character developed in different media (bronze, wood and so on) the lines of the pictograph were gradually "squared up", resulting in the rectangular form in use today.

In Chinese literature the image of the sun represents solidity and brightness, and is the symbol of a benevolent king.

There are several ancient Chinese myths about the origins of the sun. One describes an era when there were ten suns that took the form of birds, who lived in a big tree at night, and flew to light the sky during the day. Because they all shone at the same time, the ten suns scorched the fields and killed all the plants and trees, causing a famine. Luckily, a hero named Yi came to rescue the people by shooting down nine of the suns.

Another myth linking the sun to birds told that a three-legged crow lived in the sun, and so in ancient frescoes a disc containing such a bird was an immediately recognizable symbol for the sun. Later, a disc containing a bird appeared in art as part of the head-gear of a personified sun god.

Because the sun seems to move across the sky over the course of each day, the ancient Chinese also invented the myth of Kuafu, the hero who tried to race against the sun. During the race, Kuafu became so thirsty that he drank two rivers dry. He then tried to get to a large lake in the north but died of thirst before he got there.

*Ri* can also denote "day", just like the word for "Heaven", *tian* (*see p20*).

水中捞月一场空

**"Trying to fish for the moon in water is doomed to nothing."**

# MOON

## YUE

Though the moon has different phases and can be full and round, the ancient pictograph denoting this satellite of the Earth represents a waning moon. This was probably because the image served as an asymmetric counterpart to the circular pictograph for the sun (*see opposite*). The character 月 *yue* symbolizes the essence of the feminine *yin* force in nature (*see p152*), as opposed to the *yang* represented by the character 日 *ri* for sun.

Every month in the Chinese calendar starts on the day of the new moon, and the full moon falls on the fifteenth day of the month.

The character *yue*, therefore, can also denote "month" – "one *yue*" means "one month".

The Chinese believe that the full moon is largest and brightest in the middle of the eighth month of the year, so they set aside this day as the Moon Festival (also called the Mid-Autumn Festival). People celebrate this day with their family while eating specially made "moon-cakes", which are round in shape like a full moon. The festival is closely associated with the moon goddess, Chang'e, the wife of Yi, who shot down the nine suns (*see opposite*). Chang'e is said to have swallowed the elixir of immortality, which Yi

obtained from the Queen Mother of the West, and then ascended to live in the moon. Ancient myths tell of several other inhabitants of the moon, including a jade rabbit who pounds herbs for the elixir of immortality under an osmanthus tree, a three-legged toad and a man named Wu Gang, banished there because of the mistakes he made during his journey to become immortal. (*See also* OSMANTHUS, *p74.*)

The sun and the moon together are the two brightest objects in the day and night sky respectively, and thus *ri* and *yue* in combination denote "brightness".

# SPRING

**CHUN**

一年之计在于春. 一日之计在于晨

"A whole year's work depends on a good start in spring;
a whole day's work depends on a good start in the morning."

The ancient form of the character 春 *chun* for "spring" consists of grass-like elements above an image of the sun alongside a growing plant, to illustrate the coming of the season of warmth and new growth. In later forms, the grass and the plant elements were combined and abbreviated to become the modern-day radical above the *ri* radical (日) for sun.

Ancient Chinese astronomers discovered that the spring season comes when the shaft of the Plough constellation points east. They believed this change was effected by the masculine *yang* force in nature (*see p153*) returning to the world after the dark, cold winter. In ancient times, matchmaking traditionally took place in the spring months, after which girls would have to leave their homes and families to live with their new husbands, giving rise to the old saying, "Girls feel sad in spring".

The Chinese calendar divides a year into 24 solar terms, with spring starting on the first term, called *lichun* – literally "establishing spring". The Spring Festival, falling on a date between January 21st and February the 20th in the Gregorian calendar, is the most important holiday of the year and is also known as Chinese New Year. The celebratory activities of the festival include "new year visits" to relatives and friends, wearing new clothes and a family feast on New Year's Eve. In order to prepare for receiving the new year visits, every household undergoes a thorough spring clean, and decorations, mainly red in colour, are put up. Deep-fried pastry rolls containing vegetables and sometimes meat are often eaten during the festival – hence the name "spring rolls".

Spring has other, somewhat different, associations in China, because *chungong*, literally "spring-palace (pictures)", is a euphemism for erotica. This connotation derives from ancient times, when "spring palace" was usually the name of a prince's residence, and in one dynasty, the designer of an erotica album called it "Secret Plays in the Spring Palace". The label "spring palace" has stuck to this genre ever since.

# SUMMER

**XIA**

夏虫不可以语冰

**"There is no use in talking about ice with worms whose lifespan is only the summer season."**

The original meaning of the character 夏 *xia* was "people from the Central Plains", which explains the particular epigraphic form that was found engraved on bronze shown here: a figure with a torso, two hands and two big feet. *Xia* then became the name for the "Central Kingdom", serving to distinguish the Chinese kingdom from areas in its periphery, which were thought to be further away from the gods in Heaven and inhabited by barbarians. Later still, the character was borrowed to denote "summer", because the spoken word for "summer" was also pronounced *xia*.

In the traditional Chinese calendar, summer begins on the day when the sun enters the seventh solar term along the ecliptic, which falls around May 5th, and this term is called *lixia* – "establishing summer". According to the Chinese doctrine of the Five Phases, summer corresponds to the direction south and the colour red. In ancient times, therefore, all the officials in Chang'an, (the then capital city, now called Xi'an) would gather in the early hours of the first day of summer in the southern suburb, wearing red clothes to welcome the season.

There are numerous Chinese legends that evoke the heat of summer. One tells of the measures a king took to constantly remind himself that his country had fallen and that he must stay determined to save it. He slept on a firewood bed, drank gall bile and brushed fire with his hands in the heat of summer. Another tale describes an emperor's jealousy toward one of his courtiers, who was very handsome and had an admirably white face. The emperor suspected that the courtier used powder to whiten his face, so on a hot summer's day he made the courtier eat a bowl of scalding hot noodle soup. To the emperor's great disappointment, the flooding sweat on the courtier's forehead did not spoil the appearance of his face. Instead, when wiped with a silk napkin, his face shone even brighter.

**FOLLOWING PAGES, LEFT:** *Flowers and Insects* **by the Qing dynasty painter Yun Bing (active 1670–1710). The inscription, in running script, is a poem praising the colour and beauty of the flowers.**

**RIGHT:** *Peonies and Rock* **by the Empress Dowager Cixi (died 1908). Here, the running script inscription describes the flowers' fragrance and states that they came from Luoyang, a city famous for its peonies.**

雪裏春前都耐寒深黃
淺絳鬥江干清涼凡豔
余擬俗繪出憑人著眼
看
女史憚氷

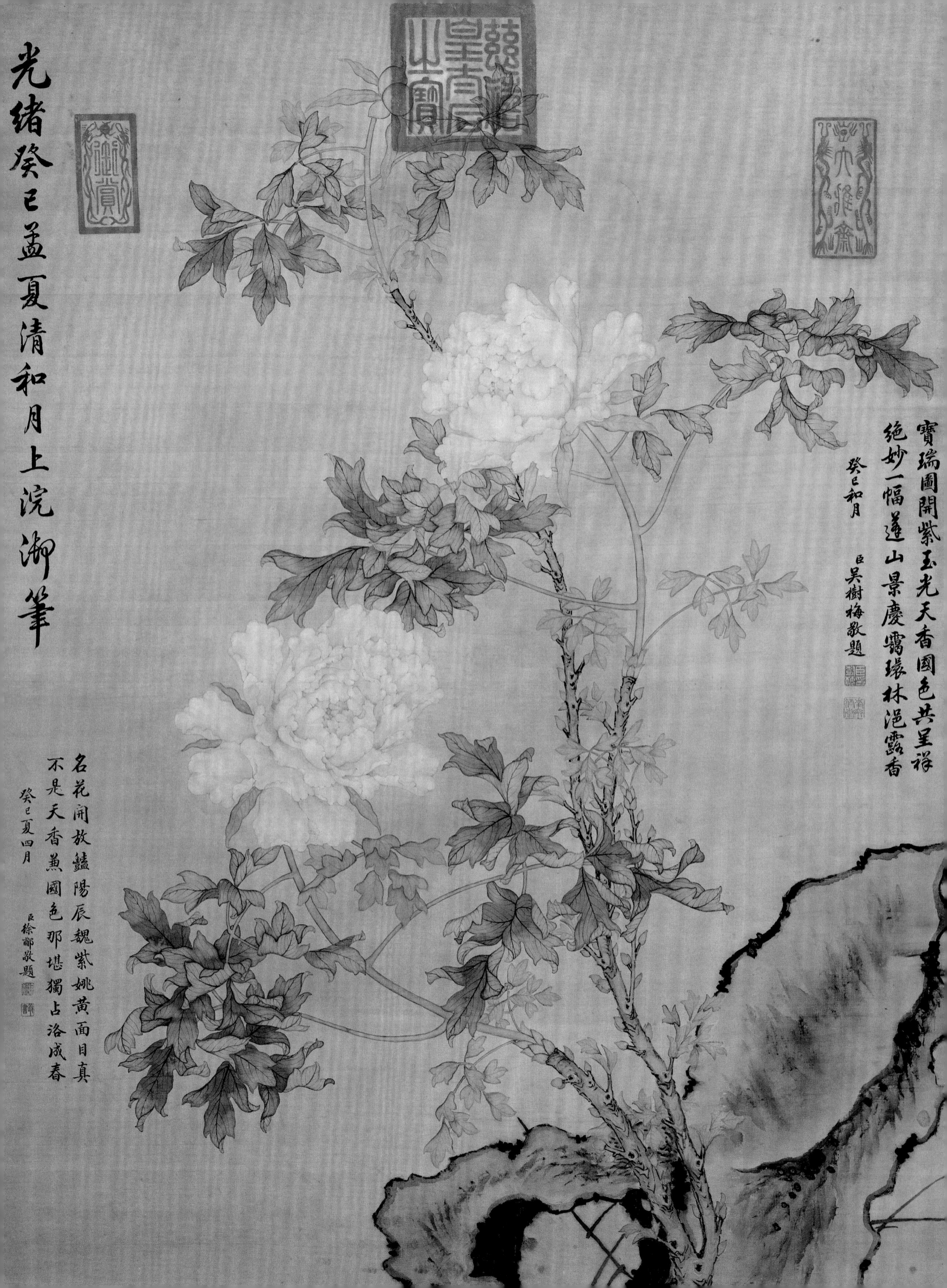

光緒癸巳孟夏清和月上浣御筆
慈禧皇太后之寶
御賞
大雅齋
寶瑞圖開紫玉光天香國色共呈祥
絕妙一幅蓬山景慶靄環林浥露香
癸巳和月
臣吳樹梅敬題
名花開放豔陽辰魏紫姚黃面目真
不是天香兼國色那堪獨占洛成春
癸巳夏四月
臣徐郙敬題

# AUTUMN
## QIU

一叶落而知天下秋

**"One may sense the advent of autumn
from a falling leaf of the season."**

One epigraphic form of the character 秋 *qiu* for "autumn" vividly depicts an insect being scorched by fire, which alludes to the Chinese agricultural practice of burning the fields in autumn after harvest, in order to kill the pests and turn the stalks into fertilizer. Later scripts clearly retain the "fire" radical at the right-hand side.

In the traditional Chinese calendar, the autumn season starts on the day when the sun enters the thirteenth solar term along the ecliptic, which falls around August 7th. This term is called *liqiu* – "establishing autumn". According to the Five Phases, autumn corresponds to the direction west and the colour white. And so, in ancient times, all the officials in the capital Chang'an (now Xi'an) would gather together in the early hours of the first day of autumn in the western suburb wearing white clothes to welcome the season.

In China, an "autumn fan" became a well-known metaphor for women who were "past their shelf life", after Ban Jieyu (ca. 48BCE–ca. 6BCE), a concubine of Emperor Cheng of Han (reigned 33BCE–7BCE), compared herself to a fan discarded after the summer heat has passed in her famous poem "Lament of the Autumn Fan". Ban Jieyu, who was also known as "Lady Ban", failed to produce an heir for the emperor and then lost his favour to two sisters who arrived in the harem. Lady Ban wrote the poem to express her sorrow, using the metaphor of a new piece of cloth being made into a fan and cherished by the user only for the summer. The poem ends: "When cool breezes overcame the summer heat, the fan was put away into a box, and affection turned into indifference all of a sudden."

# WINTER
**DONG**

The earliest form of the character 冬 *dong* for "winter" is in the shape of a length of rope with a knot at each end to symbolize the "end", and in particular, "the end of the year". In the form found inscribed on a bronze vessel that is shown here, the rope is wrapped around the sun to denote that it is no longer warm in this season. In the seal script form (second from the top), the sun has been replaced with pieces of arrow-head-shaped ice, a more direct way of conveying the coldness of winter. In later forms of the character the pieces of ice were simplified into two dots.

According to the traditional Chinese calendar, winter starts on the day that the sun enters the nineteenth solar term along the ecliptic, which falls around November 22nd. This term is known as *lidong* – "establishing winter".

Most of China, especially the north, experiences harsh winter temperatures and conditions, and it is therefore unsurprising that there is a Chinese fable about a special cure for chapped hands and feet in the winter. A family discovered a remedy for chapped skin and kept it a secret for generations, making a humble living by selling the remedy to manual labourers who had to work with icy water. One day, a wise man came to offer the family one hundred taels (the ancient currency and weights system) of gold for the cure, which they accepted. This man then took the remedy to the King of the Wu Kingdom, who happened to be at war with the Yue Kingdom, and were fighting across a freezing river. The remedy eased the Wu soldiers' chapped hands and feet, which in turn helped them to win the war against the Yue. The wise man was later enfeoffed, becoming a nobleman, in gratitude for his contribution to his country.

天不为人之恶寒而辍冬

**"Nature will not spare people the winter, just because they dislike cold."**

# MOUNTAIN

## SHAN

山中无老虎，猴子称大王
**"The monkey reigns in the mountains when the tiger is absent."**

The epigraphic form of 山 *shan* for "mountain", found inscribed on a bronze vessel, clearly depicts three prominent mountain peaks. The character then developed into the more linear seal script form before its last organic trace was discarded and the standard form, with only vertical and horizontal strokes, was finally established.

The Chinese have always been keen observers of mountains and so, just as the Eskimos have many words for different kinds of snow, they invented many specific mountain-related characters. There are characters for a wide and high mountain, a narrow and high mountain, a low and wide mound, a mountain with a large top and a small base, a vegetation-covered mountain, a bald mountain, a soil-based mountain, a stone mountain, a gathering of small but many peaks, the mountain foot, back and front, and three different characters for the peak!

According to Chinese mythology, during the creation of the Earth the creature Pan Gu's body parts became the Five Great Mountains of China. They are situated in the five cardinal directions of Chinese geomancy, which are north, south, east, west and the central point between them. Among the Five Great Mountains, Mount Tai, in Shandong province in the east, is the most famous. Believed to be sited at the location of Pan Gu's head, it was here that the emperors used to come to worship Heaven.

Daoism considers mountains to be sacred because they are seen as numinous columns that connect Heaven and Earth. Daoists believe that at a mountain's summit one can receive refined cosmic energy, gather herbs and minerals for longevity elixirs, and even encounter immortal masters. Because of their spiritual significance and physical beauty, mountains were, and still are, frequently subjects of Chinese paintings. Indeed, the Chinese word for landscape painting is *shan shui hua* ("mountain-and-water painting"). (*See also* PAINTING, *p148*.)

# FIELD

**TIAN**

瓜田不纳履,李下不整冠

"It is advisable not to tie your shoes by a melon field, nor to adjust your cap under a plum tree, in case you look suspicious."

*Tian* (田) belongs to the small number of present-day characters that have continued to bear a close resemblance to the ancient pictographs from which they ultimately derive (this category of characters, known as *xiang xing*, also includes 山 *shan* for "mountain", and 日 *ri* for "sun"). In fact, the origin of the form of *tian* – a field divided into plots for agriculture – is so clear as to require almost no explanation. Traditionally, land has always been divided into small units in China, so that it is easier to manage them, and to distribute them among tenant farmers.

Chinese farming practices date back to at least Neolithic times – evidence suggests that woodland was being cleared for fields as early as 10,000BCE. Since then, the great majority of Chinese people have lived in villages, scattered for the most part across the vast agricultural basins of the Yellow and Yangzi Rivers. In the plains of the Yangzi delta, the traditional checkerboard panorama of rice paddies is broken only by the occasional small hill crowned with a dense thicket of gravestones.

It was said that fields first appeared in China during the reign of Shen Nong (believed to be 2737–2697BCE), the second of the Three Sovereigns – the legendary first rulers of China. He is supposed to have invented the plow and the hoe, established the uses for all different kinds of plants and crops, and created the first markets for selling them. *Huainanzi*, a philosophical treatise of the 2nd century BCE, describes how "in ancient times, people ate grasses and drank from rivers; they plucked fruit from trees and ate molluscs and beetles. At that time there was much suffering from illness and poisoining, so Shen Nong taught the people for the first time how to sow and cultivate the Five Grains [*wu gu*: panicum and setaria millet, soybean, wheat and rice]." (*See also* FARMER, *p96.*)

**LEFT: Rice fields in Long Ji, Guangxi province, southern China.**

# RIVER

**CHUAN**

子在川上曰，逝者如斯夫，不舍昼夜

*Confucius stood by a river and said,* "Everything in the world flows like this, without ceasing, day and night."

The earliest form of the character 川 *chuan* for "river", found inscribed on oracle bones, depicts a river, with islets and whirlpools, confined between two banks. Its later forms more directly resemble flowing rivers, perhaps running toward the sea.

The world's third longest river is in China, called Changjiang (which means literally "long river"). The lower reaches of this vast waterway came to be known as "Yangzi" around the 6th century. When the Europeans visited China they encountered this part of the river first, and thus the whole river's name came to be "Yangtze" in English. Today, the Yangtze valley is the most important economic zone in China, with Shanghai at its mouth by the sea.

The second longest river in China is the Yellow River, on whose plains the many historic capital cities of various provinces that it crosses have sprung up. The river is considered, therefore, to be the "cradle of ancient Chinese civilization". The name "Yellow River" came about because the water contains a high level of yellow-brown silt, which comes from its source in the Loess Plateau. The silt also causes the riverbed to be high, making the water change its course frequently and resulting in flooding in the surrounding plains – earning the river the alternative name of "China's Sorrow".

Flooding rivers have caused much suffering in China's history, and several people who played a role in combating floods became national heroes. For example, Yu the Great (ruled 2205–2197BCE) is remembered for mastering flood control technology and leading his people to fight against floods. An advisor to the King Li (died 828BCE) of the Zhou dynasty even used flood control as a metaphor of the king's rule, telling him: "A water course needs to be dredged often to prevent it from bursting its banks; people need to be given freedom of speech in order to prevent the accumulation of anger."

**The Li River in Yangshuo, Guangxi province, southern China. Known for the traditional cormorant fishing that takes place on its waters, the river flows down from the Mao'er Mountains of Xing'an into a tributary of the Pearl River in Wuzhou.**

# SEA

## HAI

海不让水，积小以成其大

**"The sea is infinite because it does not refuse even the tiniest stream that runs into it."**

The epigraphic form of the character 海 *hai* for "sea" shows clearly a "water" radical (水) at the left-hand side, to indicate that the meaning is related to water. The right part of the character is, in fact, a character that means "wild growth of grass", and is there to indicate how this character would originally have been pronounced.

For the ancient Chinese, the sea was the heavenly pond that linked all the rivers under the sun, and a symbol of ultimate vastness. A fast drinker in China is described as being like a "whale sucking up the sea", while a heavy drinker can be said to have the "capacity of the sea".

The first inland Chinese peoples established the idea that the sea was far, far away and, therefore, that anything "on the other side of the sea" was considered definitely alien. As a result, *hai* is often present in the names for things that were "foreign". Plants brought to China from the West were named with the character for "sea" at the beginning of their compound, such as *hai-tang* for crab-apples and *hai-liu* for pomegranates, both of which were imported fruits of non-Chinese origin.

In the *Analects*, Confucius's pupils quoted their teacher's well-known saying, "All men living within the Four Seas are brothers." While this may sound like a declaration of global unity, the definition of the "four seas" in the first Chinese thesaurus *Er Ya* is "areas inhabited by various barbarian tribes in the peripheries of the Central Plains", and so Confucius's saying actually means, "All those living on the Central Plains (of China) are brothers."

# WATER

## SHUI

水能载舟，亦能覆舟
**"While water can bear the boat, it can also sink the boat."**

The oracle bone form of the character 水 *shui* for "water" shown here resembles a current moving through a series of pebbles and boulders. This was one of a few different epigraphic forms that existed for "water" before the Qin dynasty (221–207BCE) when the character became regularized in the seal script form. From then on *shui* became a widely used radical for many water-related characters, such as *hai* for "sea" (*see p40*).

Admired for its life-sustaining ability and hidden strength, water is an important symbol in China. According to the Five Phases, water corresponds to the colour black, the direction north, the season winter, the planet Mercury and the organ kidney. Laozi, the founder of Daoist philosophy, famously observed that water "is the softest substance under Heaven, but it can drive through even the hardest substance."

Water is also the first mirror in which humans were able to see themselves. However, ancient Chinese sages stressed that a true gentleman should regard his peers as his mirror *before* water, because although he can see his face in water, he will be able to "see" his fate and future in the opinions of his peers.

Confucius once observed, "The wise man finds joy in the forever-changing appearance of water, while the benevolent man appreciates mountains", and according to Chinese philosophy, the contemplation of water and mountains in nature is vital to the well-being of the spirit. Landscape paintings were often used as a substitute for contemplating nature directly, and they were named *shan shui hua*, literally "mountain-and-water" paintings (*see also* PAINTING, *p148*). A 12th-century essay, "The Lofty Power of Forests and Streams", captures the orthodox Chinese view of *shan shui hua*, stating that when an artist recreates nature on paper, he should not only imitate the appearance of the scene but also convey its mood. Moreover, if he is a court painter, the artist must eulogize imperial order itself, by picturing the mountains and water in a painted scene as natural expressions of a higher, cosmic order.

薪尽火传

**"Even though one piece of firewood is burnt,
the flame will still pass on to the next."**

# FIRE

**HUO**

The simple image of a rising flame with sparks flying out from either side is easily discernible in the ancient form of the character 火 *huo*, and is still in the form adopted today, which has hardly altered over the centuries.

The second of the Five Elements, fire plays an important role in traditional Chinese life. In addition to its essential and obvious practical value, it also has symbolic significance, as the means by which humans can communicate with the gods and ancestors – burning incense, paper effigies and "spirit money", which ascend in the form of smoke to those in the heavenly realm.

Fire can also represent speed, danger, anger, ferocity – a nimbus of fire surrounds the fierce deities of Buddhism – as well as joy, lust and strength. As the embodiment of heat, fire represents the season summer, the direction south and the red planet Mars, the "Fire Star". Moreover, fire's colour is red – the most auspicious of all.

Danger, anguish and joy, all concepts associated with fire, meet in childbirth. In some parts of China, therefore, a bride was sometimes carried over a burning brazier, or sometimes a red hot ploughshare, which was placed on the threshold of her husband's house. This was said to ensure that the bride would successfully overcome the perils of labour.

When the Chinese first invented gunpowder sometime late in the first millennium CE, the substance was mainly used in another Chinese invention – firecrackers and rockets. Today, firecrackers still accompany celebrations for Chinese New Year and many other traditional festivals, crackling with festive joy and supposedly driving away malign spirits.

The radical for fire appears in numerous combinations to form new words. A volcano, straightforwardly enough, is a "fire mountain" (*huo shan*). But anger is "fire breath" or "fire wind" (*huo qi*) and a spark is a "fire flower" (*huo hua*). The word for train is "fire vehicle" (*huo che*), which vividly conveys the impression that steam locomotives must have made when they first arrived in China.

# WOOD

## MU

木从绳则直，君从谏则圣

**"If the carpenter follows the ink lines laid on a piece of wood, he can cut it straight; if a king follows the sensible advice of his courtiers, he can be a sage king."**

The epigraphic form of the character 木 *mu* for "wood" clearly illustrates its original meaning – "tree", with a fork-like tree head at the top and fork-like roots below. In its seal script form, the upper and lower "forks" were stylized into curves. In the later stages of the character, the top curve evolved into a simple flat bar and the lower curve into a pair of left and right calligraphic strokes.

Trees and wood have fulfilled various roles in Chinese daily life throughout the ages. They have been one of the primary building materials and fuels, and have also provided a surface for decorative art and ornament. However, they are also of important symbolic interest – according to the Five Phases, wood corresponds to the colour blue, the direction east, the season spring, the planet Jupiter and the organ liver.

Ancient Chinese thinkers were keen observers of nature, and some paid particular attention to the forms and life histories of trees. They tried to draw wisdom from their observations, often expressing them in sayings that are accessible to us today. The great philosopher Laozi wrote more than two millennia ago, "Even a tree of colossal size starts from a tiny seed," emphasizing that even the grandest enterprise can have a humble beginning. Another Daoist philosopher, Zhuang Zi (ca. 4th century BCE), once found a tall, leafy tree standing alone, and on being told that the tree was of no use to carpenters commented, "This tree has had a peaceful long life simply because it is no use as a source of wood."

# SOIL

**TU**

积土成山

**"Soil can be accumulated to form high mountains."**

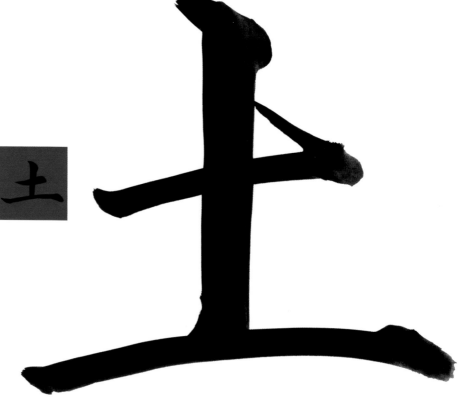

The simple image of raindrops falling on a sprouting shoot provides the form for the earliest character for 土 *tu*, meaning "soil", "earth" or "dirt", and also "ground" or "land". This epigraphic form developed into the more strictly linear strokes of the present-day character.

The original pictograph says much about the importance of the fertile soil of China's plains and river deltas, which was being cultivated as early as 10,000BCE, and without which Chinese civilization could never have flourished. According to ancient myth, it was from this same soil that the great goddess Nv Wa created the very first people, by mixing it with water and then flicking off muddy droplets from a stick. Each of these droplets is supposed to have transformed into a human being.

Even today, when millions of rural Chinese people are leaving the countryside for the rapidly expanding cities, China remains a land of farmers, especially in the inner provinces. Turning virgin ground into fields for crops is a deeply ingrained habit. One Western traveller to Inner Mongolia in the 1940s observed that the Chinese immigrants living there would assiduously dig up uncultivated grassland near their houses and plant seeds, even though the land was much better suited to pasture.

Most traditional Chinese homes, particularly in villages, will have an image of Tu Di Gong, the local deity of the earth. He is represented in various ways, depending on the locality, but commonly as a middle-ranking heavenly bureaucrat, a benign white-haired old gentleman who is addressed affectionately as "Grandad" and is eminently approachable by all. Before a burial, prayers may be offered to Tu Di to thank him for receiving the deceased back into the earth. (*See also* FIELD *and* FARMER, *pp36 and 96.*)

# STONE

**SHI**

水滴石穿
**"Dripping water wears through rocks."**

The first two strokes of this character, reading from the top, represent the word "cliff", and the early epigraphic form of 石 *shi* can therefore be understood to represent a boulder lying by a cliff. This image can still just be discerned in the modern-day character.

Stones embody reliability and durability, and, together with rocks and mountains, they represent longevity, considered one of the principal blessings in China. A painting presented as a gift to an elder will often show a stone or rock in some form. Emperors and other important figures were often buried with stone attendants, concubines and animals to protect and accompany them in the afterlife.

Linked to this idea of the benevolence and protective qualities of stones is the ancient belief that they can drive off evil spirits, like the guardian stones often found in front of Chinese houses and other buildings, or at the junctions of streets. In some parts of China, people used to pray to sacred stones for rain, while other stones were believed to confer fertility on women, helping them to conceive sons in particular.

Stone is relatively plentiful in China, and is found in many varieties – from limestone, marble, granite and sandstone, which have been used in building for centuries, to semi-precious stones such as agate, lapis lazuli, malachite, turquoise and jade, which are often carved into ornaments and jewelry, as well as other objects. Beautiful natural rock formations were appreciated in their own right for their aesthetic value by scholars – who might keep them on their desks along with carved stones, particularly jade, in the likeness of sacred mountains. (*See also* JADE, *p138.*)

# LONG DRAGON
## LONG

龙游浅水遭虾戏
**"The dragon in shallow water will be teased by shrimps."**

The original vigorous, twisting pictograph amply conveys the dynamic serpentine form of a dragon, a dynamism that can still be sensed in the modified present-day character – 龍 *long*.

The fifth creature of the Chinese zodiac, the *long* dragon is one of the most complex and multilayered of all Chinese symbols. Its ferocious energy binds together all the phenomena of nature: bringing benevolent rain, but also typhoons; shaping the landscape, and causing earthquakes. One of the guardian creatures of the cardinal directions, the *long* dragon stands in the east, the source of the sun, spring rain and fertility.

*Long* dragons appear in several different forms in Chinese mythology – those with scales are called *jiao long*, those with wings *ying long*, those with horns are *qiu long*, and small-sized ones are *chi long*. Despite their ferocity, these mighty beasts are also fundamentally beneficent, the most auspicious of all creatures and embodiments of masculine vigour and the concept of *yang* (*see p153*). Because of these associations, the dragon, particularly one with five claws, was the symbol par excellence of the Chinese emperor, the Son of Heaven, and is often found embroidered on imperial robes. It is also the embodiment of the land – quite literally at times, for the features of the landscape were seen by some to be the features of an enormous dragon. This dragon would sleep under the earth during the winter, then ascend to the skies on the second day of the second month, bringing the first spring thunder and rain. For masters of feng shui, underground currents are the veins of this great dragon, and therefore ought not to be disturbed by human builders.

Because of its auspicious and imperial associations, many Chinese place names contain the word for dragon, such as the Hong Kong town of Kowloon, which means "nine dragons" (*gau lung* in Cantonese, *jiu long* in Mandarin). This refers to eight local hills, known as "dragons", while the ninth "dragon" was the boy Emperor Zhao Bing (reigned 1278–1279), last ruler of the Southern Song dynasty.

**LEFT:** Emperor's yellow court robe (*chaofu*) in silk gauze, from the reign of the Qing dynasty emperor Kangxi (ruled 1661–1722). This detail shows the imperial symbol of a five-clawed dragon.

**FOLLOWING PAGES:** *Nine Dragons*, dated 1244 (detail), by the Southern Song dynasty painter Chen Rong (active ca. 1235–1262).

# FENG PHOENIX

**FENG**

宁当鸡头，不做凤尾
**"It is much better to be a chicken's head than a phoenix's rear end."**

The character 鳳 *feng*, for the mythical Chinese phoenix, derives from an oracle bone pictograph depicting a bird with a crest and claws, with a sound element (pronounced *fan*) above, which means "the most general thing". In the seal and later script forms of the character this sound element is much larger, and encloses the bird image on three sides.

The *feng*, or *feng huang*, which is often portrayed to resemble a peacock or golden pheasant, is the second of China's Four Sacred Creatures (the others being the *long* dragon, the *qilin* unicorn and the tortoise). Except in its mythic status, this creature is not related to the fabulous fire-born bird of Mediterranean and Near Eastern mythology. However, the *feng* phoenix *is* linked with heat, since it is the guardian of the south, and therefore a symbol of the sun, summer warmth and harvest. The Chinese phoenix is sometimes interpreted as a male (*yang*) animal, but when accompanying the (male) *long* dragon it represents a wife, and pictures of a dragon and phoenix together symbolize marital bliss. As the imperial *long* was a symbol for the emperor, the *feng* was the particular emblem of the empress, and a woman on her wedding day might wear a dress adorned with the phoenix to show that she was "empress for the day".

In Chinese literature, the body of the phoenix is sometimes said to represent the Five Good Qualities: virtue (the bird's head); humanity (the breast); reliability (the stomach); duty (the wings); and proper ritual conduct (the back). Like the *long* dragon, the *feng* has important imperial associations. It was said to appear only during the reign of good, just emperors; and, unsurprisingly, artists and poets commonly flattered their imperial masters by declaring that a phoenix had been spotted on their land. Confucius, on the other hand, in his day bemoaned the absence of the phoenix and other auspicious celestial signs.

# CRANE

**HE**

鹤立鸡群

**"Like a crane standing among chickens."**

According to the oldest dictionary in China, the *Shuo-wen jie-zi* (*Explanations of Simple Graphs and Analyses of Composite Graphs*), the earliest character for "crane" consists of a symbol for a bird, the present-day 鳥 *niao*, at the right, with feet and a feathered tail, along with a sound element at the left indicating how the character should be pronounced.

With the exception of the legendary phoenix, the crane is the most auspicious of all birds in China, and a highly popular creature in mythology. One of the most common symbols of longevity (cranes were reputed to live for six hundred years), the bird is often depicted in the company of other symbols of great age, such as a pine tree, a rock or a peach (*see also* LONGEVITY, *p174*). The high-soaring crane represents gentlemanliness and is also supposed to carry away those who have attained immortality. In addition, the way in which its young echo their parent's song makes the crane a symbol of the dutiful relationship between children and parents (*see* FILIAL PIETY, *p178*). Indeed, under the Ming and Qing dynasties (1368–1912), the most senior grade of imperial civil servants – the highest-flying, oldest, wisest and most dutiful "sons" of their imperial "father", the emperor – wore an image of a white crane as their badge of rank.

The crane is also regarded in Chinese mythology as the psychopomp, the bearer of the soul to the afterlife. At traditional funerals the coffin might bear the image of a crane with outstretched wings, ready to carry off the spirit of the deceased to the celestial paradise of the western mountains.

According to legend, the famous Yellow Crane Tower, originally built in 223CE in the city of Wuhan, marks the spot where a Daoist priest drew a dancing crane on the wall of a tavern in gratitude for free hospitality; to the wonderment of all, the picture came to life and danced. A later legend recounts that a scholar standing on the tower asked a crane for a ride; when the bird agreed, the scholar was borne away to the Western Paradise, never to be seen again.

**LEFT: Silk-embroidered official badge of a high-ranking civil servant showing a white crane, dating from the late 17th century, during the reign of the Qing dynasty emperor Kangxi (ruled 1661–1722) .**

# DEER

## LU

鹿死不择庇荫

**"The deer being driven to death will have no need to try to find the best place to rest."**

The earliest pictograph of the character 鹿 *lu* for "deer", while by no means anatomically correct, exhibits the most clearly recognizable characteristics of the animal, showing the four legs, slender head and body, and prominent antlers. Pared down over the centuries, the head and legs are still just visible in the modern-day character.

A deer represents wealth in China, owing to the fact that *lu* ("deer") is a homophone of *lu* ("official income" or "emolument"). A gift of a painting showing a deer alongside an imperial official is a way of wishing the recipient advancement in officialdom.

Deer were reputed to live for a very long time and hence, like cranes and tortoises, they are symbols of longevity (*see p174*). For this reason deer antlers are a highly valued ingredient in many preparations of traditional Chinese medicine, and are reported to prolong life, aid virility and alleviate various ailments. An illustration of these medicinal properties is found among the *Twenty-Four Examples of Filial Piety* compiled by Guo Jujing during the Yuan dynasty. According to one of the stories, there once was a boy, referred to as Tanzi ("Young Master Tan"), whose parents suffered from an eye disease that could only be cured by drinking deer's milk. Observing a herd of does and their young, the couple's son donned a deerskin and crept among a group of fawns as they suckled their mothers. In this way, Tanzi was able to collect a bucket of deer milk and bring it to his delighted mother and father. He repeated the ploy every day for many weeks until their sight was restored. The son's devotion came to light when a hunter almost shot him one day by mistake. Luckily the boy stood up just in time to reveal his disguise.

# TORTOISE

## GUI

龟三千岁，蜉蝣不过三日，以蜉蝣而为龟忧养生之具，人必笑之

**"Tortoises have a life of 3,000 years, while mayflies have only three days. It would be laughable for a mayfly to be worried about how a tortoise can live a healthy long life."**

The side profile of a tortoise, complete with feet and shell, is still discernible in the modern-day character that denotes the animal (龜), and can easily be traced back to its very literal, early pictographic form. The examples here show how, over time, the shapes of the tortoise's body have become more stylized and approximated, most notably in the markings on the shell, now abbreviated into a cross.

Together with the *long* dragon, *feng* phoenix and *qilin* unicorn, the tortoise is one of China's Four Sacred Creatures, and the only one of the four that is a real animal. Tortoises are able to live to a great age, and are a symbol of longevity, wisdom and the ability to foresee the future. According to myth, the creator goddess Nv Wa used the legs of a giant cosmic tortoise to support the sky after the collapse of the mountain that had previously held up the heavens. Because of their identity as load-bearers and their association with longevity, carved tortoises are commonly used as supports for funerary inscriptions.

Tortoise plastrons, or undershells, were often used by the diviners of China's ancient Shang kings (17th–11th century BCE). The diviner pressed a hot rod onto these "oracle bones," "read" the meaning of the resulting cracks, and inscribed it on the bone or shell. These inscriptions constitute the oldest extant Chinese characters (*see pp7–9*).

According to legend, tortoises were indirectly responsible for the invention of Chinese writing. The mythical creator of Chinese characters, Cang Jie (*see p6*) is supposed to have spotted a tortoise while out hunting. The creature's fascinating anatomy prompted Cang Jie to devote himself to the study of nature and the cosmos, and then to devise the first symbols that would represent natural elements.

Tortoises have negative connotations, too, being linked with female infidelity as well as illegitimacy. This arose from a former belief that all tortoises were female, and mated with snakes. An illegitimate person might therefore be called "child of a tortoise".

# FISH

**YU**

临渊羡鱼，不如退而结网
**"Do not stand by the water and long for fish;
go home and weave a net."**

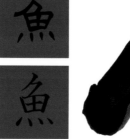

A head, scaly body and tail are clear to see in the ancient, pictographic form of 魚 *yu* meaning "fish". These original strokes have since been reduced almost beyond recognition. The fish's tail, for example, is now represented simply by a series of dashes.

A fish is an ancient symbol of material prosperity and fertility in China, both because another word pronounced *yu* means "abundance", and because of the huge quantities of fish in Chinese lakes and rivers. In some parts of China, people would eat the flesh of fish, and then offer the heads as a sacrifice to Zhao Gongming, the god of wealth.

The invention of fishing is often attributed to Fuxi (believed to have reigned 2852–2737BCE), the first of the Three Sovereigns – China's mythical earliest rulers – and fish has certainly been a staple of the Chinese diet for millennia. Fisherman was one of the respected Four Occupations for common people, the other three being peasant farmer, woodman and scholar.

Fish is a common dish at festivals, especially Chinese New Year, when the fish is served with its head and tail intact, indicating a wish for prosperity from the beginning of the year to the end. Keeping goldfish in the house is considered auspicious, since the name for "goldfish" (*jin-yu*) puns on the Chinese words for "gold" and "jade" as well as the phrase "abundance of gold".

Goldfish, and fish in general, are often found as decorative motifs in Chinese art. A fish and a lotus together signify "wealth for all the future" by a double wordplay, because a fish symbolizes wealth and a lotus (*lian*) is associated with the Chinese phrase *lian nian* meaning "year in, year out". Fish swimming in water are thought to be joyful and so represent a happy marriage, as well as sexual intercourse.

Carp sometimes swim upriver, against the current, and are, therefore, emblems of perseverance associated with those commoners who struggle to pass civil-service examinations in order to enter a different social arena. (*See also* OFFICER, *p101*.)

**RIGHT:** *Flowers and Insects* by the Qing dynasty painter Yun Bing (active 1670–1710). The running script inscription describes the happiness of these water creatures in the Hao river, an allusion to a famous story called "The Happiness of the Fish" in the ancient Daoist text the *Zhuangzi*.

點水萍綠亂牽風行帶長落
紅吹不定幽趣在濠梁

牛不喝水强按头

**"One cannot force an ox to drink by pushing its head into the water."**

# OX

**NIU**

Little altered from its ancient pictographic ancestor, the character 牛 *niu* for "ox", or "cow", represents a buffalo's head viewed from the front, with its horns and ears protruding from a central axis.

Traditionally, cows were so crucial to the Chinese farming economy that it was considered disrespectful to eat them, a disinclination that persists to this day, probably reinforced by Buddhism, which promotes vegetarianism. At times, imperial decrees actually outlawed the slaughter and eating of oxen, and until the end of the Chinese empire they were central to the ceremonial act of ploughing that marked the beginning of spring. The emperor himself took part in this rite, behind an iron-tipped ox-drawn plough, dressed in splendid imperial yellow robes. This was one of the most important national rituals of the empire. Elsewhere, clay models of an ox were beaten in local ceremonies intended to encourage the onset of spring.

The Chinese word *niu*, like "ox" in English, is a non-specific term, usually taken to refer to the "yellow ox", the most common East Asian cow. Preceded by the word for water (*shui*), it denotes the water buffalo, an animal particularly revered in the south of China.

Unsurprisingly, the ox is an important symbol of strength and patient endurance. Statues of oxen, such as the bronze water buffalo on the banks of Kunming Lake at the old imperial Summer Palace in Beijing, were believed to ward off malign and disruptive spirits.

The Ox-Herding Sequence is one of the most famous subjects of Chinese Chan (Zen) Buddhist art. Popular during the Song dynasty (960–1279), the sequence of ten verses accompanied by drawings represents the quest for enlightenment, using the metaphor of a plain herdsman (the seeker) in search of an ox (the enlightened mind).

路遥知马力，日久见人心

**"A long journey proves the stamina of a horse, the passage of time reveals the true nature of a person's heart."**

# HORSE

**MA**

The character 馬 *ma* originated in its oracle bone form as the outline of a horse's profile. The later seal script form abbreviated the body of the horse to a line and later still the head tilted and the prominent eye diminished, giving way to an approximation of a horse's mane. In the present-day character, this mane is standardized into three horizontal bars and the four legs approximated by four dots (or a wavy line in more cursive forms).

No animal has exercised as much influence over the destiny of China as the horse, which was central to the power of the various mounted nomadic peoples who dominated north China during the Period of Disunion (220–581CE), and the entire empire under the Mongols (Yuan dynasty, 1279–1368) and Manchus (Qing dynasty, 1644–1911). The long *queue* (tail) of hair, which all Chinese males were obliged to wear under the Qing emperors, is said to have been inspired by the horse's tail – an ever-present reminder to the emperors and their Chinese subjects of the animal on which their armies had swept down into China, ousting the native Ming. Indeed,

it was the Chinese who – possibly borrowing the idea from nomads – first invented stirrups, making riders more stable and agile, and cavalry a more efficient weapon of war. Before then, in ancient China, horses had been prized primarily as fast draught animals, pulling swift coaches for the wealthy, and chariots on the battlefield. Other wheeled transportation was drawn by oxen.

Ceramic models of horses produced during the Wei dynasty (386–557CE) were much admired and imitated by later Chinese artists, and the sport of polo, which was imported from Iran, became popular among the cosmopolitan aristocracy of the ensuing Tang dynasty (618–907CE).

A horse's much-admired swiftness and power are reflected in its classification under the element fire, and it is also therefore associated with the direction south. The difficulty of taming and riding a frisky horse may account for the term "horse-will," used in the famous novel *Journey to the West* by Wu Cheng'en (ca. 1500– ca. 1582) to describe a headstrong and impulsive nature.

# DOG

## QUAN

The character 犬 *quan* for "dog" is not far removed from its pictographic origin, a simple but immediately recognizable portrait of an animal with the erect ears and high, curling tail that marks out the sturdy chow chow and other common breeds found in China. This image has been balanced into near symmetry over the course of its development to reach the form in use today.

Dogs are held in high esteem in China as faithful guardians, and to be approached by a dog is said to herald great riches. Emperor Ling of the Eastern Han dynasty (ruled 156–189ce) was so fond of his favourite pet dog that he bestowed upon it the highest rank of a scholar, and gave lesser ranks to his other dogs. In the late empire, the small lapdogs now known as Pekinese were highly popular at the Qing court in Beijing (then Peking).

In the north of China dogs are seen as protectors against evil. Pairs of Dogs of Fo (meaning "dogs of the Buddha") – also called lion-dogs – were placed at the entrances to Buddhist temples, and miniature versions became popular during the Qing dynasty to ward off ill-fortune in houses and other buildings. Blood from a dog, perhaps one that had been slaughtered for

food, was also commonly used to cure demonic possession. In southern China the dog is even more revered, especially among minority peoples of the far south, such as the Yao, who claim that a dog is the ancestor of humankind. However, dogs can also be considered as bringers of bad luck. In Taiwan, dead dogs were, until recently, often disposed of in water because it was believed they would become demons if buried.

Dog features on the menu in various parts of China, and in the south the chow chow – revealed by DNA research to be one of the oldest breeds of dog in the world – is among those especially fattened up for the table.

画虎不成反类犬

**"He who sets out with the overambitious idea of portraying a tiger ends up with the likeness of a dog."**

# ELEPHANT

## XIANG

Elephants are no longer native to China, but the recognizable legs, trunk, ears and tusks of an Asiatic elephant in the early character testify to the fact that the animal was once found widely in the Middle Kingdom – mainly in the south but also occasionally in the northern regions.

The mythical Emperor Shun, one of the exemplary first rulers of China, is said to have been helped by an elephant to plough his fields, in recognition of his filial deeds. Ancient Chinese rulers used elephants in battle, and they have long been symbols of strength, prudence and wisdom. The elephant, lion, leopard and tiger together constitute the Four Powerful Animals of Chinese legend.

The elephant's reputation as a sagacious creature no doubt owes much to a strong association with Buddhism, which reveres the animal as sacred. On the eve of his birth, the Buddha is said to have descended from the Tushita heaven, one of the Buddhist paradises, into his mother's womb in the form of a six-tusked white elephant. The precise moment at which he would then have assumed human form was much debated by Buddhist scholars. In China, artists resolved this issue, when depicting the Buddha's descent from Tushita, by combining elephant and human forms

– depicting a tiny human Buddha riding on an elephant's back – as befitted one who was to be born a royal prince.

Unsurprisingly, given such an array of positive symbolism, elephants were closely associated with the Chinese emperors. The tombs of several rulers of the Ming dynasty (1368–1644) are approached by a long processional causeway, or "spirit path" (*shen dao*), that is lined by monumental statues of elephants and other emblems of imperial might and wisdom. Richly caparisoned elephants are also depicted among the entourage of the Kangxi emperor (ruled 1661–1722) and other rulers of the Qing.

人心不足蛇吞象
**"A man whose greed is never satisfied is like the snake that wants to swallow an elephant."**

# PINE

## SONG

岁寒，然后知松柏之后凋也
*Confucius said,* **"It is only when winter comes that we realize pines and cypresses are evergreen."**

The character for pine is a combination of the radical that originally meant "tree" (木) and an element (公) that means "urn", indicating the word's pronunciation.

The pine is held in high regard in Chinese tradition and appears in Chinese art and poetry more frequently than any other tree. It is evergreen and can withstand the harshest winter weather – hence, along with firs and cedars, pines represent constant friendship and endurance in adverse times. Pine, bamboo and plum (*see pp66 and 72*) are the Three Friends of Winter and together symbolize the ideal scholar, who is steadfast in all weathers – political or otherwise.

Above all, the pine is an emblem of longevity, and is commonly depicted together with other symbols of long life or immortality such as cranes and peaches (*see p174*). In Chinese, the word for "nine" is a homophone of "forever", and therefore to give someone a picture of nine pine trees and nine cranes expresses a wish that the recipient will be blessed with great age. According to ancient Chinese texts, taking pine resin can actually extend a man's life – he will feel lighter and energetic, his teeth will remain intact and his hair will stay black.

The association of pine with eternity probably explains why these trees are commonly planted at graves. However, the pine tree was also traditionally believed to repel the *wangxiang*, a ferocious hungry demon that eats the brain and liver of the deceased.

Pines and firs are widely planted in gardens as ornamental trees, and dwarf pines are the most popular trees grown in *penjing*, the miniature gardens more widely known in the West by the Japanese version of this name, *bonsai.*

**Pine trees in heavy fog, Huangshan mountains in Anhui province, eastern China.**

# BAMBOO

**ZHU**

竹篮打水一场空
**"Drawing water with a bamboo basket will achieve nothing."**

In the current form of the character 竹 *zhu*, the image of two bamboo stems side by side is still clear. Other ancient forms of the character show the pair gently bending toward one another, illustrating the flexibility of this highly esteemed plant. "Young bamboo bends easily" is one of the many common sayings that refer to bamboo, and no other plant features so often in Chinese folklore, song and art.

Bamboo's popularity derives primarily from its usefulness, and this fast-growing plant – although in fact it is technically a grass – is still put to a vast range of uses in China. It is useful almost as soon as it starts growing – young shoots are eaten as a delicacy, while thick, mature stems are used as scaffolding, which may seem precarious to the Western eye but in fact is strong and supple. It was once the main raw material for writing – paper being made from bamboo strips, and bamboo stems of varying widths being made, as they still are, into brush handles and pots. So revered was this plant that porcelain brush pots were often made in imitation of their bamboo counterparts.

Bamboo represents youth and suppleness, but also old age, because it is long-lived and evergreen – it is one of the Three Friends of Winter, together with the pine and plum. The word for bamboo, *zhu*, is a homophone for "wish" and the plant is therefore also depicted in art to reinforce wishes for a range of blessings.

Bamboo's noble characteristics derive from its ability to bend with the wind while remaining firmly rooted. It therefore represents humility and endurance (sometimes depicted by bamboo with a rock), while the hollow centre symbolizes an open heart that is able to learn. These are historically the virtues of the *literatus*, the gentleman scholar-official, who is often pressured to bow to the wishes of his masters and is subject to the whims of the political climate.

**LEFT: "Leaf J", from** *Tian Jingzhai mozhu ce* **by Rang Tian (ca. 18th–19th century). One of twelve loose leaves in an album, each depicting bamboo. Signed by the artist in cursive script and stamped with his seal.**

# LOTUS

## LIAN

莲出淤泥而不染
**"The lotus comes out of the mud unsoiled."**

The character 莲 *lian* for lotus was created by placing two plant-like elements on top of a sound element – a composite character meaning "man-pulled vehicle" (連).

The lotus enjoys great significance in the arts and traditions of China and many other parts of South and East Asia, because of its close association with the Buddha. Growing up through the murky water from the muddy depths, the pure and undefiled lotus flower finally emerges and unfolds its multiple petals in the light – a process by which the Buddha described the path of the mind from ignorance and dim awareness to clarity and enlightenment.

The lotus is one of the Eight Auspicious Signs in Chinese and Tibetan Buddhism, and as a symbol of enlightenment it is often found in Chinese Buddhist art and especially the Sino-Tibetan style that was patronized by the Yuan and Qing emperors, who practised the Tibetan form of Buddhism. The Buddha and a host of other enlightened beings, such as the popular Chinese goddess of mercy, Guanyin, are commonly portrayed in two- and three-dimensional art sitting or standing on a stylized lotus-flower support. As a symbol of purity and perfection the lotus is also important in Daoism, and is the particular attribute of He Xiangu, one of the Eight Immortals of Daoist tradition.

Another reason for the popularity of the lotus in Chinese art is the several homophones of *lian*, which also means "love" and "bind together" – making the flower an emblem of marriage – as well as "uncorruptedness" and "unbroken sequence". Felicitous combinations of the lotus with an additional element are thus virtually endless. For example, a lotus (*lian*) together with a fish (*yu*) expresses a New Year wish for plenty (*yu*) without interruption (*lian*). The many seeds in the lotus seed pod also suggest a wish for many offspring.

**FOLLOWING PAGES:** "Lotus Flower" from *An Album of Flowers* by Shou-Ping (1633–1690). The inscription, in running script, is a couplet that likens the flower to a lady whose face has been freshly made up, as well as to Lady Yang, the famous consort of Tang emperor Li Longji.

雲歸巫女妝猶潤

浴出楊妃睡未醒

南田

# PRUNUS

## MEI

望梅止渴

**"One's thirst can sometimes be quenched by just imagining the sourness of a plum."**

The tree commonly referred to in English as the flowering plum in fact belongs to the species *Prunus mume*, which is part of the apricot family. The epigraphic form of the character 梅 *mei* for "prunus" is an image of a large plum on top of a tree, with the radical for "tree" above. In the extant seal script form of the character there is a sound element at the right-hand side that means "flourishing grass".

With the pine and bamboo, the plum is one of the Three Friends of Winter, symbols of strength and endurance. Unlike its fellow plants in this group, the plum is not an evergreen, but it enjoys a special significance as the first tree of the year to blossom, even before the cherry. The briefly-flowering pretty red, white or pink blossoms – which appear before the leaves – signify the imminence of spring, and are emblems of hope, as well as of beauty, virginity and the fleeting nature of existence.

Furthermore, the plum, bamboo, chrysanthemum and orchid constitute what are traditionally known as the Four Gracious (or Gentlemanly) Plants. The five petals of the plum blossom also symbolize the five elements (wood, fire, earth, metal and water), and the Five Happinesses.

The prunus acquired great popularity as an artistic and poetic motif from the Song dynasty onward, a period when China was threatened and subsequently, under the Yuan (Mongol) dynasty (1279–1368), governed by foreign invaders. For the traditional Chinese scholar-artist, the dilemma of whether to work for the new dynasty and risk being viewed as a traitor, or to withdraw from official life and risk persecution and penury, was a common theme, often necessarily expressed through subtle symbolism. Plum blossom signified courage in adversity – "braving the frost", as the 11th-century poet Wang Anshi put it – and, in times such as the Yuan era, the hope of better political times to come.

**LEFT: Detail from a porcelain bowl showing a prunus branch, dating from the Yongzheng period (1723–1735). Enamalled predominately in shades of purple and pink, this style of porcelain was known as "Famille Rose".**

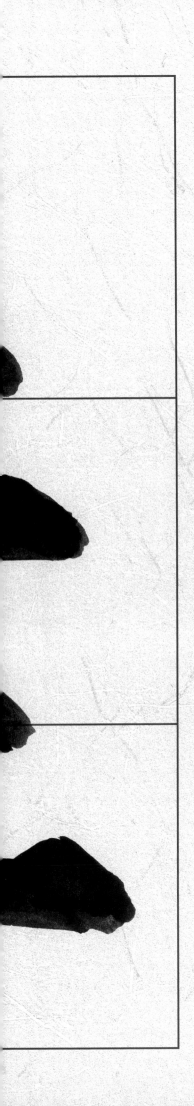

# OSMANTHUS
## GUI

蟾宮折桂

**"Plucking an osmanthus branch in the Moon Palace symbolizes passing civil service examinations with flying colours."**

The character 桂 *gui* for the sweet osmanthus is a compound of *gui* meaning "an auspicious jade ornament", to indicate the pronunciation, and the radical for "tree" (木) at the right side.

Widely popular in China and throughout East Asia, the ornamental sweet osmanthus (*Osmanthus fragrans*), also known as the sweet or fragrant olive, is a variety of evergreen shrub or tree that bears highly scented flowers, ranging in colour from white to yellow-orange. They are added to black or green tea leaves to make *gui hua cha*, fragrant osmanthus blossom tea.

The osmanthus depicted alongside another highly valued flower, the orchid, signifies the next generation of males – sons and nephews.

The osmanthus tree features in a story from the 9th-century book *You Yang Za Zu* (*Assorted Notes From Youyang*). A man named Wu Gang offends his master while learning to be an immortal and as a punishment is sent to the moon to cut down an enormous osmanthus tree. However, each time Wu Gang lifts his axe after striking the tree, the cuts immediately close, making the task as futile as that of Sisyphus's uphill stone-rolling in Greek mythology.

According to one Chinese legend there is an osmanthus tree in the courtyard of the palace in the moon – home of the goddess Chang'e (*see also* MOON, *p27*). The phrase "plucking an osmanthus branch in the Moon Palace", as quoted in the proverb above (also sometimes incorrectly translated as "plucking a branch of laurel" or "cassia"), is much the same as being a "high flier" or having "reached for the skies", and therefore meant attaining top marks in the imperial civil service examinations – usually the guarantee of a successful career.

The name of Guilin, a beautiful city in Guangxi province, means "osmanthus forest", and the plant is also an emblem of Hangzhou, one of China's ancient capitals. Hangzhou and Shanghai both have an annual autumn festival dedicated to celebrating the fragrant osmanthus flower.

# 人類

MANKIND

生　死　魂　人　心
眉　祖　母　子　夫
婦　王　士　農　工
兵　臣　家　史　祭
禮　法　樂　酒　葬
采　射　言　解

生于忧患而死于安乐
**"One survives in worries and calamities but
perishes in ease and comfort."**

# LIVE

## SHENG

The image of a plant sprouting from the ground is vividly displayed in the early pictograph for the present-day character 生 *sheng*, which means "to live", "life", "living" and "lifetime", as well as "to grow", "give birth" and "produce".

As a term referring to life in general, *sheng* is used in a number of common terms such as doctor (*yi sheng*, literally "heal-life"). The Buddhist concept of rebirth, in which many Chinese people believe, is *chong sheng* ("twice-life").

On the Shang oracle bones (*see pp7–9*) the ancient form of *sheng* often appears in requests to the ancestors for women to become pregnant, and terms relating to birth and the beginning of life remain an important aspect of the many meanings of the word. "Birthday" is *sheng ri* and "Happy Birthday!" is "*sheng ri kuai le!*"

From the early association of the character with a newly sprouted plant comes another meaning – "raw" or "unripe". The word for student is *xue sheng*, literally one whose studies (*xue*) are unripe, not yet brought to fruition (*sheng*). In some parts of China, a popular dish eaten on the seventh day of the New

Year, consisting of raw carp, is named *yu sheng*, which literally means "raw fish". However, this plays on the fact that *sheng* also means "life" and is a homophone of *sheng* (pronounced with a different intonation) meaning "success" or "promotion"; while *yu* for "fish" sounds the same as the word for "abundant" (*yu*). The dish therefore symbolizes a typical New Year wish for prosperity, success and long life.

The Chinese mouth organ, a large wind instrument, is also called a *sheng*, and peanuts are *huasheng*. Both, therefore, feature in art as auspicious motifs alluding to "life" or "birth" and "success".

人之将死，其言也善
**"Sincere are the words of a dying man."**

# DIE

**SI**

The earliest versions of the character 死 *si* meaning "to die", "dead" and "death" clearly show the radical *ren* for a human being to the right of a radical meaning "bones" or "skeleton". In the later forms of the character, the human being element has become *hua*, an inverted form of *ren* that means "to transform", "turn" or "change" but originally signified "death" or "die", representing a person who has fallen down.

To die a peaceful and natural death is one of the traditional Five Happinesses in China, alongside wealth, health, virtue and long life. Together, these are commonly represented in art by five bats. These creatures represent good fortune in China, whereas the bird most emblematic of death is the owl, whose cry is reputed to call away the soul.

In traditional households, shortly after a death in the family, the name of the deceased is written on a wooden tablet and placed on the domestic shrine with those of the ancestors. Funerary rites must be correctly followed in order to ensure that the twin souls of the deceased do not stray from the grave and cause trouble to the living (*see also* SOUL, *p80*). Graves are regarded as the home of the dead, and the best location for a burial is carefully determined with the aid of a feng shui master. Thereafter, the site must be well tended in order to keep the spirit of the deceased content. Today, despite official efforts to promote cremation (partly to discourage "superstitious" ancestor veneration), the annual "grave-sweeping festival" of Qing Ming remains widely popular in China as well as overseas. (*See also* ANCESTOR *and* WHITE, *pp86 and 156.*)

# SOUL

## HUN

魂去尸长留

**"When a person dies, his soul leaves his body but his corpse remains."**

The Chinese traditionally postulate the existence of more than one type of soul or spirit. The character for 魂 *hun*, the *"yang* vital soul" or "cloud-soul", combines the word for "cloud" or "vapour" (*yun*, which rhymes with *hun*, and so indicates pronunciation) with the character for "ghost" (鬼). The other kind of soul is the "moon-soul" or *po*. The two types, *hun* and *po*, are said to combine to make a third entity, *shen*, the human "spirit", and all three reside in the human body: the *hun* in the liver, the *po* in the lungs and the *shen* in the heart.

While the *po* is the physical vitality, the animating force that makes one alive, the *hun* is what creates a person's character. Both are essential, but it is the *hun* that determines one's status in society and hence tends to be more highly regarded. Unlike the *po*, which is necessarily present when one is born, the *hun* takes up residence only after birth, which may be partly why Chinese tradition does not tend to view abortion as sinful.

Unless destroyed by cremation, both types of soul may be troublesome after death if the funerary rites have not been correctly performed. The *hun* originated in Heaven and will return there after death; but later it might come back, wander the Earth and cause trouble. One of the most important Chinese funerary rites, therefore, was Summoning the Cloud-Soul, which was performed just before burial. The climax of the ritual was inserting a jade plug into the mouth of the corpse, so that the *hun*, having been summoned to the body from Heaven, could not escape again. Once resident it could be properly appeased with ancestor rites and – as many Chinese continue to believe – play an active benevolent part in the lives of the living.

**RIGHT:** *Bodhisattva as Guide of Souls*, detail from a silk banner found in a cave in Mogao, Gansu province, China, dating from around the 9th or 10th century. The bodhisattva is shown leading the wealthy donor who would have commissioned the painting into the Pure Land or Paradise.

# HUMAN

## REN

人无远虑，必有近忧
**"A man who doesn't plan for the future will find trouble at his doorstep."**

The character 人 *ren* looks like a person without a head or arms. However, in its most ancient form, the character represented a standing man in profile, leaning forward slightly, with his arms held out in front of him.

Although *ren* is often translated as "man", this is not always accurate, since there are also compound words (*nanren* and *nuren*) that respectively mean "male person" and "female person" – man and woman. Another compound, *renmin* (*ren*, "person" plus *min*, "people"), renders the term "people's" as in "People's Republic" (*Zhonghua Renmin Gongheguo*); "the Chinese people" is *Zhongguo renmin*. However, the word *ren* also occurs in words for professions that, historically at least, have been largely male preserves, such as "worker", "farmer" and "merchant". *Ren* also makes up half of the compound character for "rent" alongside the character for "field", harking back to the old Chinese system of landlords renting out lands to tenant farmers.

Throughout much of China's history the dominant ideology has been Confucianism, which is primarily a moral philosophy offering guidance on relationships between human beings (*ren*), including the ancestors (*see p86*). Confucius, known in Chinese as Kongzi or Kong Fuzi (551–479BCE), lived in turbulent times and looked to antiquity for examples of practices that would bring about social harmony and benevolent government. Ancient texts revealed to him a code of ethics and morality that emphasized the web of relationships that bound people, and the virtue of personal duty for the sake of the common good. At the heart of his teachings lay "humaneness", the word for which in Chinese is also pronounced *ren*. According to this principle, a parent should expect dutiful obedience from their child, while at the time showing their child love and care in return – a dynamic that Confucius applied to various other human relationships, such as emperor and official, and husband and wife.

# HEART

## XIN

The character 心 *xin* for "heart" derives from a fairly anatomical pictograph of a human heart, with an indication of the ventricles and emerging blood vessels.

Together with the lungs, liver, spleen and kidneys, the heart is one of the Five Organs of the body, which traditionally correspond to the Five Elements. The heart represents the element fire and is viewed as the "emperor of the human body", the source of consciousness, intelligence and thought, and seat of the *shen*, the spirit. A highly complex concept, *shen* might briefly be described as the radiant force that gives rise to all mental and physical activity. A medical manual written by the late Ming dynasty scholar Li Ting (1575) described two different hearts: "There is the physical heart of flesh and blood: it takes the form of a closed lotus flower and lies beneath the lung and above the liver. And there is also the luminous heart of *shen*, which generates *qi* [vital energy] and blood and is therefore the root of life."

In Chinese traditions of self-cultivation the heart is viewed as the crucible of a person's transformation. One early philosophical manual, the *Guanzi*, probably complied between the 5th and 1st centuries BCE, recommends stilling the heart and the breath in order to establish what it terms the "illumination of the spirit" (*shenming*).

The word *xin* is also used to render the concepts of "mind" and "feelings". *Xin* followed by the words for "reason", "scholar" and "specialist" therefore give the Chinese term for "psychologist" (*xin li xue jia*).

哀莫大于心死
**"There is no greater sorrow than a dead heart."**

# EYEBROW

## MEI

眉头一皱，计上心来
**"A ruse comes up from behind knitted brows."**

A clear pictograph of hair over an eye is the straightforward origin of the character 眉 *mei* for "eyebrow", and the basic structure of this image is still discernible in the current-day character.

Eyebrows are central to Chinese personal aesthetics, and the word *mei* is itself a homophone of the word for "beautiful" or "pretty", as well as "younger sister" and "prunus" (plum). A blooming plum tree with a magpie (*xi que*) on top expresses the wish, "May you be filled with happiness," – literally happiness (also pronounced *xi*) "right up to your eyebrows". The magpie is traditionally a bird of good omen in China, while the plum blossom heralds the spring and stands for good things to come (*see* PRUNUS, *p72*).

High eyebrows are considered particularly beautiful in China, and it was common in the past for women to shave or pluck their eyebrows off and paint them on higher up. The shape of eyebrows was interpreted as a marker of personality. For example, long, curved eyebrows were said to be a sign of moodiness or unpredictability; more prized were eyebrows resembling the wings of a moth or butterfly. During the reign of the Tang dynasty emperor Xuanzong (712–756CE), women would shave off their eyebrows and paint them on in the form of the Chinese character for the number eight (八), considered a highly auspicious number.

Long, overhanging eyebrows on the other hand, are revered as a sign of advanced age. Lao Shouxing, the god of longevity (*see p174*), is a very familiar figure who is easily recognizable by his long eyebrows, whereas dark, bushy eyebrows and a beard characterize portraits of Bodhidharma (*Da Mo* in Chinese), the celebrated Indian master who brought Chan (Zen) Buddhism to China in the 6th century CE.

# ANCESTOR

**ZU**

光宗耀祖
**"Bring honour to the family and win glory for the ancestors."**

The main element in the character 祖 *zu* for "ancestor" is *qie* (且), which represents the male sexual organ, reflecting the mainly patriarchic nature of ancestor worship. A radical meaning "gods and ancestors" (示) was later added, giving the character its current compound form.

Over 3,000 years ago, as oracle bones testify, Shang dynasty kings were asking their diviners to find out what would be auspicious offerings for their ancestors – the answers included oxen, pigs and even humans. Today, in traditional China, a family will continue to include its ancestors as present, vital and active members of their household, who are honoured and bound to the family by rituals, which can be understood as acts of filial piety (*see p178*). In their simplest form, such ancestor rites involve the burning of incense, in the mornings and at night, and reverential bows before a portrait of the ancestor or a wooden tablet bearing the ancestor's name. More elaborate ceremonies take place on special days, such as the anniversary of a family death, weddings, funerals and festivals. The popular spring festival of Qing Ming (literally "clear brightness"), held two weeks after the spring equinox, is also known as the "grave-sweeping festival", because it is on this day that families visit cemeteries to celebrate the lives of deceased relatives and clean their graves. It is also a popular time for entertainment and family fun, in expectation of the springtime.

While on Qing Ming the living visit their dead ancestors at their graves, conversely on the Ghost Festival, on the fifteenth day of the seventh lunar month (known as "ghost month"), the dead visit the land of the living. At this time ancestors are honoured and provided for by offerings of food and other material goods that they might need in the afterlife. In ancient times real items were offered, but today paper effigies are burned and sent to the afterlife in the form of smoke. Specially printed paper bills ("ghost money") have long been popular, and today these are often accompanied by paper houses, cars, televisions, refrigerators and even DVD players.

**LEFT: Qing dynasty ancestor portrait of a civil official's wife wearing dragon robes (late 18th–early 19th century). Carefully observed portraits such as this one were often commissioned by families to worship and commemorate their deceased relatives. To capture the details of costume was especially important because they served as symbols of the subject's social status and court rank.**

# MOTHER
## MU

慈母手中线，游子身上衣
**"The thread in a doting mother's hand
becomes the clothes of her travelling son."**

The addition of breasts to the kneeling figure depicted in the ancient character for woman (*nu*) creates the pictograph for "mother" (母 *mu*) – literally a woman who suckles. In pre-modern China the primary duty of any woman was to marry and produce sons for her new family. She was always subservient to her husband and mother-in-law, and also confined to the home – literally so if her feet had been bound. (*See also* WIFE, *p91*.)

If a woman succeeded in producing sons her status was raised considerably, because it meant that in due course she, too, could become a mother-in-law – the most powerful female in the household. Also, according to Confucian precepts of filial piety, the respect of children for their parents was the cornerstone of a stable society, and therefore a man's reverence toward his mother should take precedence over his love for his wife. At least half of the stories in the *Twenty-Four Examples of Filial Piety* demonstrate the loyalty and obedience of children toward their mothers, stepmothers or mothers-in-law (*see also* FILIAL PIETY, *p178*).

Despite the inferior status of women in traditional society, there were two occasions when exceptionally forceful mothers succeeded in effectively ruling China. The first was when Wu Zetian deposed the emperor, her own son, in 690CE, declaring her own dynasty and ruling for nearly 20 years. More than 1,000 years later, the dowager Empress Cixi, an imperial concubine like Empress Wu, effectively ruled China from 1861 to her death in 1908, during the reigns of her son Muzong and nephew Dezong.

There are several popular maternal deities in China, such as Xi Wang Mu, the powerful Queen Mother of the West (*see* WEST, *p167*), and Guanyin, the embodiment of maternal love and kindness (*see p172*).

# SON

## ZI

知子莫若父

**"No one knows a son better than his father."**

A baby with arms flung upward, and of indeterminate sex, forms the earliest pictograph for th character 子 *zi* for "son". Some early forms show the baby's two legs as well; however, these were eventually joined in a single stroke as shown here, making the character reminiscent of a baby swaddled from the waist down, a common practice in traditional China.

There is great cultural significance in the fact that this character, which actually means "child" or "offspring", is how one also renders the word "son" – in contrast, there is no non-compound character for "daughter". Throughout Chinese history, sons have been traditionally valued more than daughters, and notwithstanding official legislation on the equality of women, this attitude persists widely to this day. It was a major obstacle to the "one child" policy of the People's Republic, because parents whose first child was a girl would often risk prosecution in order to try for a son. As a family extended into the past, through its ancestors, it was also considered of foremost importance that the family extend into the future, and the begetting of male heirs was an inescapable duty. Sons guaranteed the survival of the family name, and, as breadwinners, would ensure that their parents were looked after in old age. The obedience and reverence of sons toward their fathers (and forefathers) was *the* crucial relationship in society, mirrored in the relationship of citizens toward their rulers. The emperor himself revered both his earthly father and, as the Son of Heaven (Tianzi), his celestial one. (*See also* FILIAL PIETY, *p178.*)

Motifs expressing a wish for male children abound in Chinese tradition. Chopsticks (*kuaizi*) fastened over a bride's door meant, "May you have a son (*zi*) quickly (*kuai*)." Similarly, chestnuts (*lizi*) depicted with dates (*zao*) signify, "May you soon (*zao*) beget (*li*) sons (*zi*)."

# HUSBAND
## FU

一日夫妻百日恩
**"One day of married life fosters a hundred days of attachment."**

The original pictograph for 夫 *fu*, meaning husband, depicts a man wearing a large hairpin, which in ancient China was a sign of male maturity and, therefore, of marriageable age. The character in current use is almost identical to that of 人 *ren* ("human" or "man", *see p82*), but with two horizontal strokes added, one representing the hairpin, and the other the arms.

*Fu* is a homophone of another Chinese word *fu* meaning "wife" and of yet another *fu* meaning "submissive" (*see opposite*); and also of *fu* meaning "wheat" or "bran". Grain is one of the numerous symbolic plants that play a role in traditional Chinese weddings. At one time, all marriages were arranged by parents through a matchmaker, and the prospective husband and wife had no say in the matter. In fact, if a man and woman fell in love it was often seen as a hindrance, since they might then choose their marriage partner according to their wishes and not, as filial devotion demanded, those of their parents. A prospective bridegroom was rarely even acquainted with his wife, and, once their names were known to each other, etiquette demanded that they avoid contact until their wedding day.

A husband was responsible for all matters affecting a family's relations with other families and the outside world. Apart from this, his primary duty was filiality, which meant demonstrating his reverence for his parents and ancestors by supporting the family and perpetuating the family name by fathering sons. According to Confucian principle, a husband's loyalty to his parents and clan should take precedence over any feelings for his wife, and if she fails to produce boys this is sufficient grounds for divorce. Alternatively, the husband might take a concubine in order to guarantee the next generation of males. While monogamy has generally become the norm in Chinese society today, a husband could at one time have as many concubines as he could afford, a custom that took a long time to die out. A husband might also discard, without redress, a concubine who bore him no sons.

# WIFE

## FU

巧妇难为无米之炊

"Even the cleverest housewife cannot make a meal in a kitchen where there is no rice."

According to one traditional explanation, this character (婦) was given the sound *fu* in order to remind a wife to be submissive (*fu*) to her husband (*fu*). In practice, the words for husband and wife are pronounced with different tones, however, and are rarely confused. The oldest written forms of "wife" combine the radical for "woman" (a kneeling figure, as in *mu* for "mother"; *see p88*) with a broom or rag-duster – indicating a wife's domestic duties.

In China, a bride to be was borne from her home in a "bridal chair" to the bridegroom's house, where the couple would see each other for perhaps the first time. The ceremony itself was very simple: the bride and groom bowed to his ancestors, then to his parents, and were then considered husband and wife. On the wedding night, if the wife appeared not to be a virgin, she might immediately be sent home in shame.

Footbinding – tightly wrapping and compressing the feet of girls from as young as the age of four – produced the tiny "three-inch lilies", much prized by marriage brokers, that once confined most Chinese wives to the home. The custom was officially banned after 1911 but there are victims of this agonizing practice still living in China today.

For a woman, obedience to her own parents before marriage was followed by obedience to her husband's parents after marriage. The wife was ultimately under the control of her mother-in-law, who might make her life a misery or become a lifelong friend.

There were compensations for the restricted life of a traditional Chinese wife, especially if she fulfilled her primary duty of bearing sons, which meant that she in turn might become a mother-in-law. Wives also traditionally managed the household affairs, as is often still the case today.

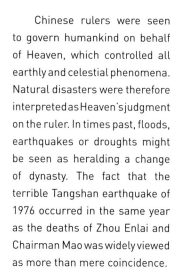

# KING

**WANG**

胜者为王败者寇
**"Conquerors are kings; the beaten are bandits."**

The form of the simple character 王 *wang* meaning "king" has changed little throughout the ages. Composed of the number three (三) connected by a vertical line, it represents the one who connected the Great Trinity of *tian di ren* – Heaven, Earth and humankind. Scholars know that this was the original symbolism because Dong Zhongshu (ca. 179–104BCE), who as a chief minister in the Western Han dynasty (206BCE–8CE), was partly responsible for establishing Confucianism as state orthodoxy, stated in his treatise *How the Way of the King Joins the Trinity*, "Those who in ancient times invented writing drew three lines and connected them through the middle, calling the character 'king'. The three lines are Heaven, Earth and humankind, and that which passes through the middle joins the principle of all three."

Before the 3rd century BCE, China was divided into a number of rival states governed by kings.

The kings of the Shang, the oldest historic dynasty, were essentially high priests, whose every act was preceded by divination and sacrifices, offered chiefly to the Shang ancestors. These ancestors were regarded as potent deities, who alone could intercede with the high god Di, or Shang Di, on humans' behalf. It is these divination rites that produced the great quantities of "oracle bones", inscribed with the earliest extant Chinese characters (*see pp7–9*).

China's states were eventually united under the First Emperor, Qin Shi Huangdi, whose reign began in 221BCE. This new role ,"emperor", was akin to a "grand king" and the Chinese character meaning "emperor", 皇 *huang*, was originally composed of the radical for king, and that for "beginning".

Chinese rulers were seen to govern humankind on behalf of Heaven, which controlled all earthly and celestial phenomena. Natural disasters were therefore interpreted as Heaven's judgment on the ruler. In times past, floods, earthquakes or droughts might be seen as heralding a change of dynasty. The fact that the terrible Tangshan earthquake of 1976 occurred in the same year as the deaths of Zhou Enlai and Chairman Mao was widely viewed as more than mere coincidence.

**RIGHT:** *Emperor Wu Di* **from a series of portraits of past emperors attributed to the Tang dynasty painter Yan Liben (ca. 600–673), dating from ca. 650–670. The inscription, in standard script, states that Wu Di reigned for 18 years in the Northern Zhou dynasty (557–581), and that he, along with the four emperors who preceded him, destroyed Buddhism.**

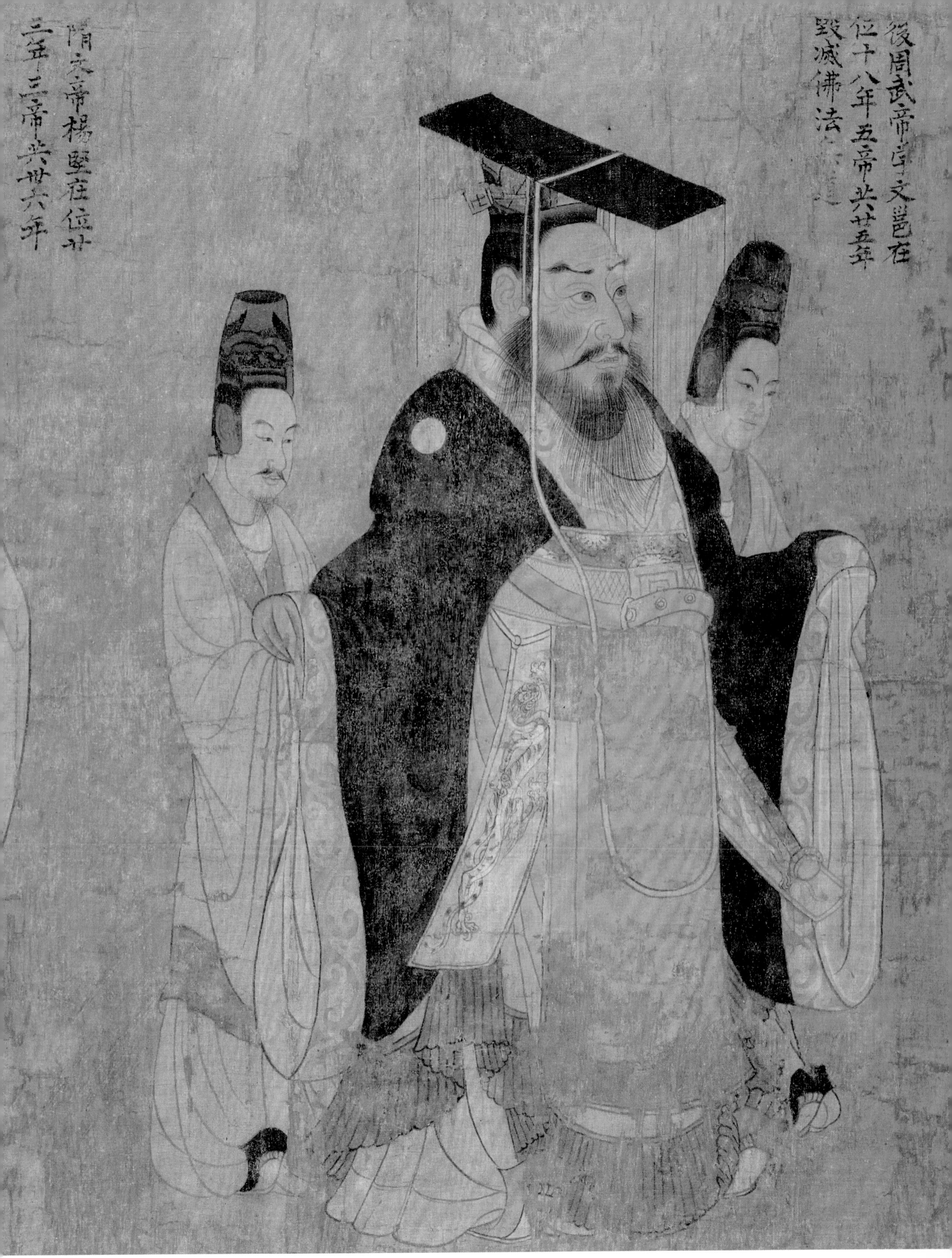
後周武帝宇文邕在
位十八年五帝共廿五年
毀滅佛法
隋文帝楊堅在位廿
三年三帝共卅六年

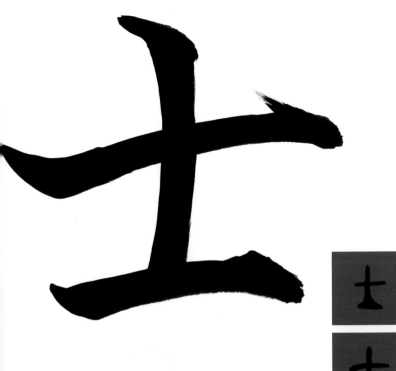

# SCHOLAR

**SHI**

士为知己者死
**"A learned man will die for an understanding friend."**

**LEFT:** *Emperor Xian Di with Scholars Translating Classical Texts*, dating from the 17th century, by an anonymous Qing dynasty artist.

The character for intellectual or scholar, 士 *shi*, is made up of the numbers one (一) and ten (十). The Chinese word for "ten" is also pronounced *shi* and this element functions partly as a pronunciation guide; however, it also means "complete", resembling a compass showing the four cardinal directions and thus representing the cosmos. In this context the combination of one and ten therefore symbolizes a "person who understands everything" or a "literate".

Scholars, also known as the *literati* and, perhaps most accurately, as the "scholar-gentry", played a key role in traditional Chinese society. They constituted the bulk of the ruling class in both town and country, and there was a large gap in status between them and the rest of the population. The narrowest definition of a scholar-gentleman was a degree-holder, someone who had passed the tough state examinations to qualify for the imperial civil service. This examination system began in the Han dynasty (206BCE–220CE) as a means of recruiting men of talent and virtue to serve the emperor. However, true *shi* were expected to be proficient in several areas of expertise, above and beyond the examinations – for example, Su Shi (1037–1101), the famous Song dynasty scholar, was, among other things, a writer, poet, calligrapher, painter, traveller, statesman and connoisseur of food and antiques.

From the Ming dynasty (1368–1644) onward three tiers of examinations were introduced for scholars. The lowest level was the District Examination, held in a candidate's local town. A handful of those who passed then went on to the Provincial Examination, and if they succeeded they would become Promoted Scholars (*juren*) and be set up for life. Some went further still and took the top-flight Literary Examination (*dianshi*), held in Peking (now Beijing). Passing this would guarantee a good government post in the capital or provinces. The exams tested candidates on the Confucian classics, moral principles and practical administrative questions, and for the *jinshi* they also had to write poetry. This tiered examination system lasted several hundreds of years, until toward the end of the Qing dynasty in 1905.

While many scholars became wealthy and powerful officials, they were not all obliged to go into government service. Others preferred to live more quietly – especially under uncongenial or foreign regimes – and engage solely in gentlemanly pursuits such as painting, calligraphy and poetry.

# FARMER

## NONG

待农而食
**"Society depends on farmers for food."**

The epigraphic form of the character 農 *nong* for "peasant farmer" consists of pictographs for "woods", "field", "hand(s)", and "plough". In its seal script form, the character was reduced to a combination of the graphs for "hand(s)", "field" and "plough". Later, in the clerical script form, the top of the character, ie the hands and the field, was abbreviated to an unrelated character with a similar form (曲), which means a "vessel holding things".

Until recent times, the vast majority of Chinese people lived off the land, and many millions continue to do so today. Before 1949 and the start of collectivization, Chinese rural society encompassed a vast spectrum of people, from wealthy landlords to landless peasants and labourers. The bulk of the people in between were *nong* – peasant landowners or tenant farmers, who lived in villages and walked or rode donkeys and buffaloes to the fields where they worked. There were also fishermen, boatmen, carpenters, masons, spinners, weavers, carters and fortune-tellers.

According to legend, the arts of agriculture were brought to China by Shen Nong, the Divine Farmer, one of the legendary Three Sovereigns. Shen Nong is supposed to have invented the plough and the hoe, and created the first markets; also, according to one 2nd-century BCE source, he taught people how to grow the five staple grains of the traditional Chinese diet (panicum and setaria millet, soya bean, wheat and rice). Later accounts describe how nine magical wells sprang up at his birth, and he used their water to nurture grains that had fallen from Heaven. Shen Nong is also said to have classified all plants into those fit for consumption and those suitable for medicinal use, selflessly tasting each one to determine if it was poisonous. It was this tradition of empirical testing that led to his name being associated with *The Divine Farmer's Canon of Materia Medica*, a classic work on Chinese medicines by Tao Hongjing (452–536CE). (*See also* FIELD, *p36*.)

**LEFT: Farmer leading a water buffalo around a paddy field in Guangxi province, southern China.**

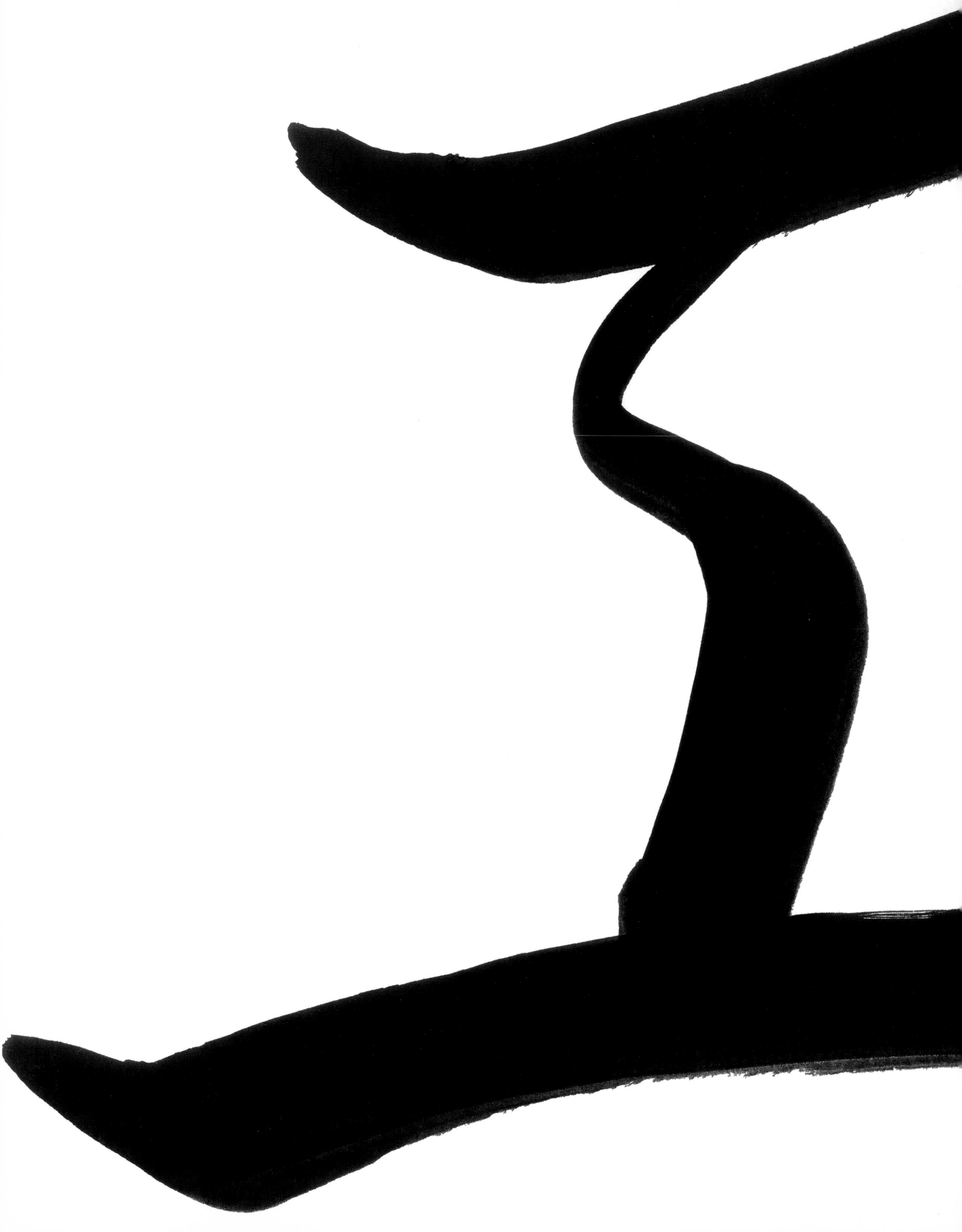

# CRAFTSMAN

## GONG

工欲善其事，必先利其器
*Confucius said*, "A workman who wants to do his job efficiently must sharpen his tools first."

Originally this character (工 *gong*) probably depicted a carpenter's "square", a simple yet essential tool for establishing right-angles in wood construction. The tool has great symbolic value in Chinese tradition, and is often depicted in images of Fuxi, the first of the legendary Three Sovereigns, China's first rulers, who is said to have reigned from 2852 to 2737 BCE. Fuxi was the supreme craftsman, and is said to have invented the square as a means to create straight lines and thus divide up the chaotic, formless universe and create the Earth, traditionally thought to be square-shaped in China.

He went on to devise nets for hunting and fishing; music and musical instruments; the Eight Trigrams (*bagua*) of divination; and the means of calculating time and distance.

From the time of Confucius (551–479 BCE) onward, craftsmen belonged to the third of the four broad sectors that Chinese society was divided into – warrior nobility (later replaced by imperial scholar-officials) at the top, farmers second, craftsmen third and merchants fourth. In this early era, an anonymous author compiled the *Kao Gong Ji* ("Records of Craftsmen"), a classic manual that set

technical standards for Chinese craftsmen including carpenters, metalworkers, ceramicists, dyers, leatherworkers and many other professions. The most important record of ancient Chinese technology, this text is a valuable source of information on Chinese mathematics as well as geography, mechanics, acoustics and architectonics, and covers the manufacturing of vehicles, weapons and musical instruments, and the building of houses and cities.

# SOLDIER

## BING

不战而屈人之兵，善之善者
**"The best general subdues his enemy
without resorting to fighting."**

The oldest form of 兵 *bing*, which means "soldier" and also "military" and "armaments", shows two hands wielding a battleaxe or similar weapon, an obvious allusion to its meaning.

Confucianists regarded war as a last resort when dealing with neighbouring countries, and believed that armies should be kept in check. The status of soldiers, particularly in times of peace, was therefore not high in the traditional Chinese social hierarchy. The military has, however, been of central importance to every Chinese ruler – from the First Emperor, Qin Shi Huangdi (ruled 221–210BCE), who was buried with an astonishing "Terracotta Army" of thousands of lifelike and lifesize pottery troops, to the three-million-strong People's Liberation Army of today, which encompasses China's ground, sea and air forces.

Owing to the threat from the warring nomads along China's long northern and western frontiers, many successive dynasties spent a large part of government expenditure on military affairs. Under the *fubing* system of the Sui and Tang dynasties, peasants were drafted into military colonies on the frontiers, and after overthrowing the Mongol (Yuan) dynasty in 1368, the Ming established a similar system nationwide. When they were not training or fighting, these troops ran their own farms. The Ming system eventually fell into decline and the dynasty was overthrown by the Manchu Banner Armies, eight disciplined units of 300 men. By the 19th century the effectiveness of these units had also declined, leaving Qing China vulnerable to foreign incursions from colonial powers.

Throughout most of imperial times, military affairs were overseen by the *bing bu* ("board of soldiers") – one of six main governmental ministries. This ministry was largely concerned with military appointments, titles, promotions, dismissals and supplies, and also ran the military examinations. Far less prestigious than the civil service tests (*see opposite and p95*), these were largely practical, involving mastery of horse riding, archery and swordsmanship. Those who passed these examinations were commissioned as field officers and might be stationed anywhere in China.

事君不弍是谓臣

**"Only an official who is loyal to his king deserves his title."**

# OFFICER

## CHEN

A figure kneeling or prostrate before his master is represented in the most ancient form of the character 臣 *chen*, meaning "official" or "minister" – one who serves the emperor or king.

From the earliest times, the success of an emperor's reign depended as much on the quality of his officials as on the calibre of the ruler. After unifying China, the First Emperor, of the Qin dynasty, laid the foundations for a nationwide bureaucracy by appointing all state officials from the centre of the country. But the capital and its surrounding areas could not supply the number and quality of civil servants needed to run an empire the size of China, so under the succeeding Han dynasty (206BCE–220CE) regional governors were ordered to put forward men of talent and virtue to serve the emperor. The selected men sat a form of examination based on Confucian literary classics and ethics. Open civil service examinations began under the Sui and Tang dynasties, and the Ming introduced the three-tier exam system that persisted until 1905. (*See also* SCHOLAR, *p94.*)

The two-tier structure of the Han government, presided over by the emperor, was inherited with occasional modifications by all the succeeding dynasties. The upper (legislative) tier drafted imperial laws and policies, which were then put into effect by officials of the lower (executive) tier, consisting of six ministries, or boards (*bu*). There were also a range of specialist agencies.

Since Han times, the basic unit of administration in China has been the county (*xian*), which in turn falls within a province (*sheng*). In imperial China each county was governed by an official called the "district magistrate", who reported to the provincial governor. This magistrate was judge, chief of police, revenue collector, and responsible for local conscripted labour and the military draft. To lessen the risk of corruption or nepotism, officials were never posted to their native district, or that of their wife.

**FOLLOWING PAGES:** *View of the Imperial Court at Peking*, **detail of a handscroll, dating from the Qing dynasty (1644–1911).**

# HOME

## JIA

家和万事兴

**"Harmony in a family is the key to its prosperity."**

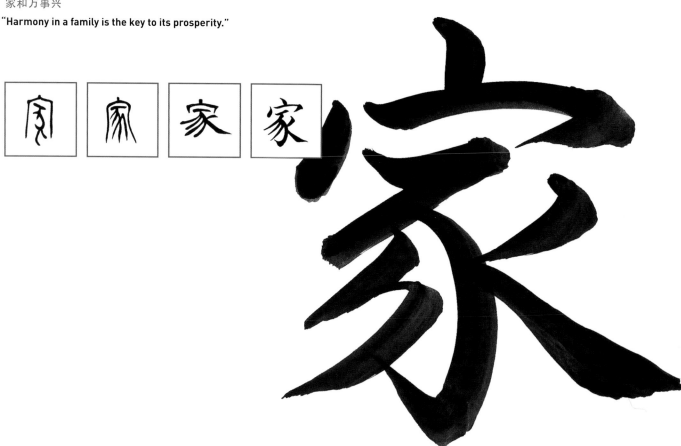

An image of a boar inside a house conveys the idea of "home" and also "household" or "family" in the ancient form of the character 家 *jia*. Animals and people shared the same roof in pre-modern China, as in some rural areas even today, and it is said that "a pig in the home means poverty, a dog riches," because a pig only eats and sleeps, while a dog protects the family and its possessions.

Traditionally, extended families of as many as five generations live under the same roof in China, and the concept of *jia* is therefore inextricably linked to that of the family. For Confucius, family was at the heart of social harmony and order, and the relationships between children and their parents, husbands and wives, living and dead, lay at the heart of what Confucianists termed *ren*, or "humaneness" (*see* HUMAN, *p82*). Among family members the word *jia* can therefore replace the possessive pronoun, and so a polite way to say "my father" is *jia fu*. In ancient times, to say that a woman had *jia* meant

that she had a husband, and in the present day a woman married, for example, to Mr Wang, can be referred to as *wang jia de*, meaning literally "Mr Wang's".

The home is at the heart of several popular traditional festivals in China, in addition to regular domestic rites honouring ancestors. The most important family festival is the New Year of the traditional Chinese calendar, when festivities last for two weeks and end with the Lantern Festival on the first full moon of the year. The family also gathers for Qing Ming, the popular "grave-sweeping festival", and the Mid-Autumn Festival, on the fifteenth day (full moon) of the eighth month of the traditional calendar. The fifteenth day of the twelfth month of the calendar marks the end of the year with sacrifices to the Kitchen God, a domestic deity who is believed to carry an annual report to Heaven on the family's conduct. (*See also* ANCESTOR *to* WIFE, *pp86–91*.)

# HISTORY

**SHI**

以史为鉴
**"History is a mirror."**

A hand holding a writing brush indicates the most ancient sense of 史 *shi* – "that which is written by a scribe". Hence this character's meaning embraces "scribe" as well as "history" and "record".

In ancient China, rulers employed scribes primarily to record official information, whether administrative or (as in the case of the oracle bone inscriptions) ritual in character. Later, scribes compiled official chronicles and annals, and some of the histories recorded became important for the moral lessons that could be gleaned from them. Two of the Five Classics – ancient texts that Confucius used to instruct his pupils – are historical writings, the *Shu Jing* (*Classic of Documents*, or *Classic of History*) and the *Chunqiu* (*Spring and Autumn Annals*). The *Shu Jing* dates largely from the 6th century BCE and records events of the Xia, Shang and early Zhou dynasties up to ca. 620BCE, as well as the deeds and sayings of legendary emperors such as Yao, Shun and Yu. Once attributed to Confucius himself, the

*Chunqiu* is the official chronicle of his own state of Lu from 722 to 481BCE. Confucius lived in unstable times and sought to convince contemporary rulers of the need for virtuous government, pointing to the examples of earlier times to reinforce his message.

The most revered Chinese historian was the imperial official Sima Qian (ca. 145–86BCE), whose classic *Shiji* (*Records of the Grand Historian*) covers two millennia of Chinese history from the legendary Yellow Emperor (*see* YELLOW, *p161*) to his own master, the Han emperor Wu Di (ruled 141–87BCE).

The importance of history was rarely lost on later Chinese rulers, including Communist ones. Mao Zedong, for example, was an admirer of the First Emperor, who united China, organized the empire and was utterly ruthless toward his opponents.

# WORSHIP
## JI

祭如在，祭神如神在

*Confucius said*, **"When one worships, one feels as if the worshipped are present. When we worship gods, we feel as if they are with us."**

A hand offering up meat to the heavens above lies behind the character 祭 *ji*, which means "worship" or "sacrifice". The character for "heavenly powers" (示), which forms the bottom part of 祭 *ji*, derives from three vertical lines representing the sun, moon and stars (the celestial powers), with two horizontal lines over the top, representing that which is above them, the heavens. It occurs as the abbreviated element (礻) in numerous other compounds, such as "ancestor" and "rites" (*see also* ANCESTOR *and* RITES, *pp86 and 108*).

The presentation of offerings such as food, drink, incense and "spirit money" lies at the heart of traditional Chinese worship, whether to the ancestors or to the wide range of popular deities and spirits. To this day many Chinese people engage in a composite religion called simply "worshipping the gods" or "religion of the gods". This amorphous and eclectic popular religion is often loosely called Daoism, but in fact its concerns and ethics – such as filial piety, loyalty, respect for authority, good deeds, compassion, longevity and preparation for the afterlife – are drawn from Daoism, Confucianism and Buddhism as well as even older traditions. The popular pantheon likewise embraces hundreds of major and local figures from all three traditions – deities, demigods, buddhas and immortals – as well as characters from legend and literature.

Popular worship is often informal in China and takes place either in local temples or, especially, in the home. At home, it is traditionally the women who ensure that regular offerings are made to the "spirit tablets" representing deceased family members, and to the family's favourite deities, such as Guanyin (*see p172*) or the Kitchen God.

LEFT: Wall hanging depicting the Buddhist view of Paradise that would have been used as an aid in prayers for the afterlife, dating from the Qianlong Period (1736–1796).

# RITES

## LI

非礼勿视、**"See nothing improper,**
非礼勿听、 **hear nothing improper,**
非礼勿言、 **speak nothing improper,**
非礼勿动 **and do nothing improper."**

The earliest form of this character depicts an ornamented bronze sacrificial vessel; later forms have the addition of a radical meaning "heavenly powers" or "gods and ancestors" (礻).

The *Book of Rites*, or *Record of Ritual* (*Li Ji*), is one of the most important of the classic Five Books, the core of the Confucian canon. Confucius believed that proper humane and righteous conduct involves the study and practice of *li*, the rituals and etiquette that he understood to be crystallized expressions of *ren* (humaneness). The *li* were so powerful that their sincere practice would bring about a transformation of the self.

In this way the *li* can be understood as a system of ethics for society to abide by for the greater good. Indeed, the Han dynasty scholar Dong Zhongshu (ca. 179–104BCE) saw the Confucian social hierarchy and a strong, unified state as part of the natural order of the universe. Crucial to maintaining this order, and national prosperity, was the correct performance of rites at all levels of society.

The emperor himself performed important annual rites to Heaven and Earth to ensure peace, fertility and a good harvest. He also made sacrifices to lesser powers such as the sun, moon, mountains, rivers and natural forces, as well as to past rulers including his own imperial ancestors, who could bestow blessings on the whole realm. State ceremonial rituals, overseen by the Board of Rites, also included sacrifices to protective deities (*shen*) who were ranked like a grand heavenly bureaucracy, from county to provincial level. Rites to a particular spirit would be performed by a bureaucrat of equal rank.

While these official rites are no longer practised, many Chinese still venerate ancestors (*see also* ANCESTOR, *p86*) and various popular deities, as well as participating in traditional rites accompanying births, weddings, funerals and festivals. (*See also* WORSHIP, *p106*.)

**FOLLOWING PAGES: Incense coils hung by devotees from the ceiling of Man Mo temple in Hong Kong. Incense has been used in Chinese ceremonies and purification rituals since as early as the 8th century BCE.**

# LAW

**FA**

法不责众

**"A law cannot be effectively enforced
when offenders make up the majority."**

The elaborate earliest extant form of 法 *fa* ("law", and also "method" or "way") consists of a stream, meaning "water", alongside the radical for "go" or "leave", shown as a person in the act of moving, as well as a pictograph signifiying "unicorn" at the right-hand side. This complex composition is believed to derive from an ancient legend claiming that a unicorn could settle a dispute by charging at the party who was in the wrong. The unicorn element was dropped in the seal script form of the character to form the basis of its current appearance.

When a student once asked Confucius how governance should work, the philosopher replied, "With moral principles and law ... If the subjects are the horse, the king is the rider, his officials the reins and laws the whips." From the earliest times China had a well-developed system of laws based on an impressive legal code, which remained remarkably constant until the end of the imperial era.

These laws were based on moral principles, which Confucius and other sages derived from practical experience. Traditional Chinese law was not seen as divinely inspired but simply as a reflection of social practice, and as such it has retained an influence even on the Western- and Soviet-inspired legal system of the People's Republic.

In ancient China, the law was seen primarily as an aid to government rather than an independent arm of the state as it is in the West. There were no judges apart from imperial bureaucrats, especially the district magistrates, and no separate legal profession. Legal matters were supervised by the Board of Punishments, a government ministry.

People of different social or family status had different penalties imposed upon them. If a son struck his father it was considered a serious breach of filial piety (*see p178*) that in extreme cases could be punished by beheading. On the other hand, if a father beat his son to death, he might be let off if judged to have been intolerably provoked. There were five grades of criminal punishment: beating with light bamboo, beating with heavy bamboo, penal servitude, exile, and death. A death sentence could be imposed only by the emperor, in whom supreme legal authority rested.

# MUSIC

**YUE**

The epigraphic form of the character 樂 *yue* for "music" is generally thought to depict drums on a wooden stand, and such instruments are among the oldest in China's long musical tradition.

In ancient China, music was one of the Six Arts emphasized by Confucius, along with rites, archery, mathematics, calligraphy (including painting) and charioteering. A central element of ritual, music was supposed to help connect sovereigns with Heaven, and the living with their ancestors.

Among the earliest evidence of Chinese music-playing are 21 bone flutes found in a tomb dating to around 6,000BCE. In 1978 Chinese archaeologists unearthed a complete ritual orchestra in the tomb of Lord Yi of Zeng (died ca. 433BCE), which included spectacular sets of 32 stone chimes and 65 bells that can still be played. The Chinese word for stone chime, *qing*, is a homophone of the word for "blessing", and is therefore a common element in pictures and other artefacts which convey "good luck".

There is a vast array of traditional Chinese instruments. The songs in the *Shi Jing* (*Classic of Poetry*), which date from the 11th–7th centuries BCE, mention nearly 30 types of wind, string and percussion instruments, including bronze

bells, stone chimes, flutes of bone or bamboo, clay ocarinas, drums, mouth organs and silk-stringed zithers and lutes. (*See also* ZITHER, *p149*.)

Central Asian and other foreign music became influential in China from the Han dynasty onward, and during the Tang dynasty (618–907CE) court music ranged from small chamber ensembles to great orchestras of 200 musicians. During the later dynasties, theatre music became popular, including the much-loved form of entertainment known as *jingxi*, or Beijing opera. Involving song, dance, acrobatics and mime, *jingxi* has its roots in shows put on in the capital for the 80th birthday of the Qianlong emperor in 1790.

乐至则无怨

**"The masses will have no complaints when they are all civilized by music."**

# ALCOHOL

## *JIU*

酒逢知己千杯少
**"A thousand toasts with a good friend are still too few."**

The oldest form of the character 酒 *jiu* shows an ancient wine vessel, to which the radical for "water" or "liquid" was later added to further emphasize the nature of the vessel's contents. This water element has, over time, been reduced to a few vigorous droplets in the current-day character.

The word *jiu*, often translated as "wine", actually refers to all varieties of alcoholic liquor, which, in China, are mostly distilled or fermented from cereals, such as rice, wheat, barley or millet, rather than from grapes and other sweet fruits as in the West. Rice wine (*mi jiu*) is rather sweet like Japanese *sake* and, like most traditional *jiu*, is drunk warm. Traditionally, it is unusual for liquor to be consumed alone, without food, although this is adhered to less strongly nowadays. Grape wine (*putao jiu*) has acquired some popularity in China since the early 20th century, but traditional liquor is still much preferred.

Alcohol is said to have been invented in the reign of Emperor Yu the Great (ruled 2205–2197BCE), the legendary founder of the Xia, thought to be China's first dynasty. The Xia capital may have been the late-third-millennium BCE site of Erlitou in Henan province, discovered in 1959, which has yielded the earliest Chinese bronze wine vessels, probably also used in ancestor rites. The cult of royal ancestors became highly developed under the Shang, who overthrew the Xia in around 1,500BCE and, like their successors the Zhou (1046–221BCE), used many types of bronze liquor vessels in elaborate ancestor ceremonies. A great number of these beautifully cast and decorated containers have been unearthed by archaeologists in recent years.

The celebrated Tang dynasty poet, Li Bai, wrote many verses about the pleasures of *jiu*, which often accompanied *literati* gatherings as well as recitals of music and verse. Today, a *jiu xi* ("liquor feast") – a large meal accompanied by drinking – is the traditional Chinese way of marking a significant personal event, such as the birth of a child, a wedding, the building of a new house or the establishment of a new business.

# BURY

**ZANG**

葬，先轻而后重；莫，先重而后轻

*Confucius said,* "If more than one person passes away at the same time, we bury the less revered first and the more revered later; when we make offerings, we go to the more revered first and the less revered later."

The earliest pictographic forms of 葬 *zang*, which means "to bury (the dead)", depict two hands tying a corpse (the same skeleton element that is present in "to die"; *see p79*), with grass-like elements on top. These symbols reflect traditional ancient Chinese burial practices, in which the body was wrapped in grass (or grass matting) and left to decay in a remote spot.

In recent decades, the government of the People's Republic has encouraged cremation over burial on the grounds of saving space, but also to discourage "superstition". However, burial still remains popular today, owing to the strong Chinese belief that a soul needs a corpse and a tomb to reside in after death. (*See also* SOUL, *p80*.)

In China, the manner of a person's burial is supposed to reflect their status in life. The *Li Jing* (*Classic of Rites*) specifies that the mausoleum of a king should be 10m (32ft) high and surrounded by pine trees, a duke's tomb 5m (16ft) high and surrounded by cypresses, a senior state official's tomb 2.7m (9ft) high and surrounded by poplars, and an ordinary scholar's tomb 1.3m (4.3ft) high and surrounded by elms. Within families a similar hierarchy of funeral rites is observed, in accordance with filial piety (*see p178*). These are most elaborate and prescriptive for the elderly, to whom due filial reverence must be shown by their descendants, often by means of the burning of incense, wailing, prayers and music. The rites are simplest for children and the unmarried, who have no one to perform filial acts for them. Infants, for example, are buried in silence, and unlike elders require no period of mourning after burial. Absence of ritual does not, of course, imply absence of grief.

Choosing a good burial site is important, so that the deceased will bestow blessings on his or her descendants from the afterlife. Cemeteries are often on hillsides, especially in rural areas, since according to the principles of feng shui, the higher the site the more auspicious it is. The "dragon vein", which correlates to the directions of mountain ranges, valleys and rivers and can be located using Chinese geomancy, is also considered lucky. After the hundred-day period of mourning observed for most family members, his or her relatives visit the grave regularly, especially on the "grave-sweeping" festival of Qing Ming. (*See also* DIE *and* ANCESTOR, *pp79 and 86*.)

# PICK

**CAI**

参差荇菜，左右采之。窈窕淑女，琴瑟友之。

**"Long and short the water fringes;
To left and right I pick them.
A pure maid, so alluring,
Like lute with zither, I will befriend her."**

The character 采 *cai*, which means "pick", "select", "gather" and also "colours", derives from a pictograph of a hand plucking fruit or vegetables from a tree or plant, an image that has remained remarkably clear through the millennia.

One of the most typical activities associated with "picking" in China is the harvesting of tea leaves by hand. Tea has been produced and drunk in China for thousands of years, for both its medicinal properties and its pleasant flavour, and the picking of the correct leaves is an essential part of the process. The 8th-century treatise *Cha Jing* (*Classic of Tea*) was written by Lu Yu during the Tang dynasty and is the world's earliest known monograph on tea. The text describes in detail when tea leaves should be picked and how they should be preserved, using special tools. These methods vary according to the seasons in which the tea plants shoot, and the resulting tea can therefore be categorized into Spring Tea, Summer Tea and so on – each possessing different qualities. Most high-quality tea is picked in early spring and made from young shoots – often just buds with a couple of short leaves. There are hundreds of different varieties of tea drunk in China today. However, they can be broadly grouped into four categories: black, white, green and oolong.

The ancient Chinese would have picked from many plants and trees, learning what was edible and beneficial. Mulberry fruit, for example, was used early on in Chinese medicine for digestive problems and to prevent hair from greying, while the leaves were picked to feed silkworms (*see also* SILK, *p134*). Similarly, some water plants were discovered to be edible, such as water chestnuts, and are still picked and included in many Chinese dishes today. Fruit grows in abundance in the Chinese climate, and the Chinese diet has always included a wide range of fruits of all kinds. It is also very common to present fruits as gifts and as offerings to ancestors and deities. Tangerines (*juzi*) are considered appropriate gifts because the *ju* syllable sounds similar to *ji* meaning auspicious, whereas dates (*zaozi*) might be left in the room of a newly-wed couple because *zao* is a homophone of *zao* meaing "early" and therefore expresses a wish for the wife to become pregnant with a son as early as possible.

**LEFT: Tea-picking in Longjing, Zhejiang province, Hangzhou.**

# SHOOT

## SHE

射人先射马

**"In order to kill the mounted enemy, you should shoot his horse."**

The earliest form of the character 射 *she* clearly represents a bow and a hand grasping the tail-end of an arrow, in preparation to shoot. Somehow, in the later seal script form, this was transformed into another existing character (身), which means "body", with a "hand" radical on its right. In the clerical script form, the hand radical was transformed into another character (寸), which, incidentally, originally signified a place on the hand between the thumb and index finger used by acupuncturists.

A bow and arrow was an important and effective weapon for hunters and warriors in China for centuries, and was recorded on oracle bones more than 3,500 years ago. Considered to some extent a nobleman's skill, archery became a compulsory component of military examinations during the Tang dynasty (618–907CE), and remained a part of military training in China until as late as 1901. Several specific manuals were written on the subject, and survive to this day, advising the archer on concentration, stance, tension of the string, and so on.

Shooting an arrow with a bow was also significant for Chinese ritual traditions (*see also* RITES, *p108*). There is some evidence of the use of archery in pre-dynastic shamanic rituals, as part of ceremonies to ask for relief from drought, and protection from invaders. Confucius was also later recorded as endorsing archery as a noble form of competition, because participants stand side-by-side and aim for a target as opposed to engaging in hand-to-hand combat. From as early as the Zhou dynasty, 1046–221BCE, therefore, archery competitions and simulated hunting exercises became an important part of court rituals.

The forms and sizes of bows and arrows themselves have changed much over the centuries. However, they were traditionally crafted from a variety of materials including bamboo, ox horn, rubber, silk thread, lacquer and bark, and were created and decorated by bowyers in specialist workshops supported by the Imperial Treasury. (*See also* BOW, *p129*.)

*She* is also present in several modern-day constructions. In football, *shemen* means to shoot at the goal (*men*, literally "door" or "gate") and in scientific terminology *she* is the equivalent of the Western prefix "radio-". Thus *fu she*, literally "shooting out like the spokes of a cartwheel (*fu*)", means "radiate" and "radiation", and *fang she* ("releasing rays") means "radioactive".

# SPEAK

**YAN**

言者无罪，闻者足戒
**"Blame not the critic but heed what he has said."**

The oracle bone form of the character 言 *yan*, for "speak", is an image of a mouth with a tongue sticking out of it. This tongue component became more elaborate in later epigraphic characters and was retained in the seal script form. In the clerical script character, however, this element was stylized and standardized into three horizontal bars.

In the strict social hierarchy and etiquette of ancient China, to speak was to risk causing offence unless one's words were carefully considered at all times, and, in general, impressive actions were more highly prized than impressive words. Confucius famously said, "Gentlemen speak with their actions, while small men speak only with their tongues."

Several Chinese sages also noted the complicated relationship between spoken words and their meaning, as well as between spoken and written words. For example, Confucius observed, "Writing cannot express everything in spoken words, while spoken words cannot express everything of what the speaker means."

The idea that speech is closely related to trust and honour is reflected in some other words that include the word *yan*. For example, combined with the character for "human" it makes the word for "sincerity" or "trust" (*xin*), rather like the idea of a person "standing by their word" in English.

# DIVIDE

**JIE**

解铃还须系铃人
**"The bell tied to the tiger's neck has to be untied by the person who did it in the first place."**

The ancient pictograph for 解 *jie* shows an ox's horn being used as an implement for prising something apart, to convey the meaning "divide" or "separate". This character is used in a wide range of terms and also refers to loosening or untying, both in a literal and figurative sense. It can also signify unravelling information, meaning "explain" and "solve" as well as "understand" and "know". An example of its use in this context is the title of the Han dynasty text the *Shuo-wen jie-zi* (*Explanations of Simple Graphs and Analyses of Composite Graphs*) compiled by Xu Shen, which was the first dictionary to analyze Chinese characters and also group them according to their shared elements.

The idea of "separating" or "dividing" is used as a Daoist metaphor in one traditional Chinese myth. In the Daoist classic *Zhuang Zi*, there is a famous fable about a master butcher who was an expert at separating (*jie*) meat from bones and was one day deboning an ox carcass for a Lord Wenhui while he watched. The rhythmic movements of the butcher's hands, shoulders, knees and feet, together with the fleeting sound of meat being separated from

the bones, delighted the lord, reminding him of the divine music and dances performed in court, and he asked the butcher the secret of his skill. The butcher told him that it was not only skill but the *Dao* (the Way) that was guiding his knife smoothly through the natural crevices between the flesh and the bones. On hearing the butcher's story, Lord Wenhui remarked, "Now I know what I should do to maintain my well-being."

Because *jie* also refers to the loosening of bonds, the phrase *jie fang* means "to liberate" or "liberation" in the social and political sense. It is the word that was used to describe the "liberation" (that is, Communist takeover) of the Chinese mainland in 1949, when Mao Zedong's forces drove out the Nationalist government of Jiang Jeshi (Chiang Kai-Shek). Mao's army, and the modern Chinese military machine that succeeded it, was called *Ren min jie fang jun* – the People's (*ren min*) Liberation (*jie fang*) Army (*jun*).

# 物體

OBJECTS

宮 車 弓 米 瓦
絲 革 金 玉 紙
筆 典 圖 畫 琴

# PALACE

## GONG

夏禹卑宫室，恶衣服，后圣不循

"The great sage King Yu of the Xia dynasty looked down upon palaces and disliked luxurious clothing, but the late sages did not follow his example."

FOLLOWING PAGES: The Forbidden City, Beijing.
So called because it was inaccessible to the public for 500 years, this palace complex was home to two dynasties of emperors, the Ming and Qing.

The character 宫 *gong* originally signified any large building, represented by a symbolic image of two rooms under one roof – in ancient China the majority of the population would have lived in single-room huts. However, since the time of the Qin, China's first imperial dynasty, the term *gong* has also denoted the residence of an emperor.

While most domestic buildings in China were generally constructed of readily available local materials (such as adobe in the north, and stone in the south and in hilly areas), palaces, official buildings, temples and wealthier houses were almost invariably made of wood. This is why so few *gong* have survived – they were generally burnt down amid the violent overthrow of one dynasty by another. The only imperial palace still intact is the Forbidden City in Beijing, which was built by the Ming in the early 15th century and remained the imperial palace until the end of the Qing, China's last dynasty, in 1911. It follows the general plan for *gong* established in the Sui and Tang dynasties, with its principal ceremonial halls built along a strict north-south axis, and subsidiary buildings – government offices, stores and accommodation – at either side.

Entrance to the complex is from the south – the chief cardinal direction (*see* SOUTH, *p165*) – through the *Tiananmen* (Gate of Heavenly Peace). Crossing a moat one enters the palace proper through the imposing *Wu men* (Meridian Gate), leading to the first courtyard of the Outer Palace, with its elegantly curving Golden Water River. Beyond this, all facing south and separated by further courtyards, are the great ceremonial halls, including the Hall of Supreme Harmony with the emperor's throne. Finally, at the north end of the main axis, lies the Inner Palace – the apartments of the emperor, his family, closest advisers and bodyguard.

车到山前必有路

**"The cart will find its way around the hill when it gets there."**

# VEHICLE

## CHE

The image of an ancient two-wheeled chariot, seen from above, remains remarkably clear in the present-day character 車 *che* denoting "vehicle". However, the pair of horses drawing the chariot was lost early on.

The first evidence for wheeled vehicles in China dates from the Shang dynasty (ca. 1500–ca. 1050BCE) with the appearance of two-wheeled chariots with spoked wheels, an import from Central Asia. By the 4th century BCE, Chinese wheelwrights were constructing well-crafted wheels with hubs, spokes – as many as 30 on chariot wheels – and sectioned rims (*felloes*).

Also around at this time, the Chinese invented the technique of "dishing" – fixing the spokes at a slight angle to the plane of the circumference, making the wheel more resistant to lateral shocks. The Terracotta Army buried with the First Emperor (ruled 221–210BCE) includes numerous superb models of war chariots, in addition to an intricate bronze model of the emperor's own travelling chariot drawn by four horses.

Before the motor age two wheels were the norm for most forms of road vehicle, whether drawn by horses, oxen or people, and, in fact, in China today, they remain the most popular mode of transportation – in the form of the bicycle.

The first steam locomotives to arrive in China in the 19th century were aptly named "fire vehicles" (*huo che*), and this remains the word for "train", whether powered by diesel, electricity or steam. *Che dao* ("vehicle way") means a lane of a highway and *che ku* ("vehicle store") is the term for a "garage". The character 庫 *ku*, which now means storage in general, originally represented a vehicle under a roof and meant a place to store a chariot or cart.

# BOW

**GONG**

引弓而不发

**"Draw the bow but do not shoot – it is a bigger threat to be intimidated than to be hit."**

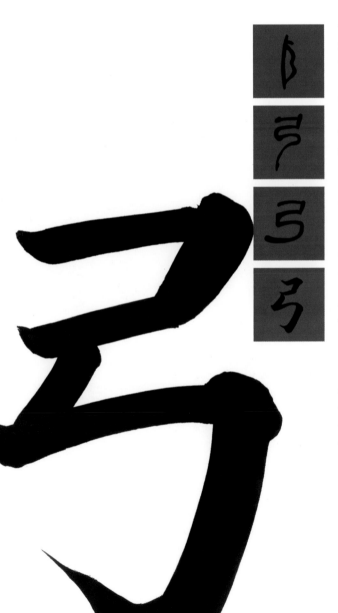

The shape of the ancient Chinese war-bow lies behind the appearance of the character 弓 *gong*, which has remained relatively unchanged over the millennia. In its oldest known form, there is a horizontal line at the top of the character that perhaps represented an arrow.

By the second millennium BCE Chinese bowyers had already developed the composite bow made of wood and one or two other materials, such as sinew and ivory laminated together, unlike the simple bow made from a single length of wood. The composite bow had greater power and was shorter in length, making it ideal for mounted use. This was a "recurve" bow, with the ends curved away from the archer, further enhancing the bow's power and creating the shape reflected in the present-day *gong* character (弓).

This technology, which probably originated among Central Asian nomads, did not appear in the West until the 2nd century CE.

The most famous bowman of Chinese legend was the divine archer Yi (or Hou Yi), who shot down nine of the ten suns, often depicted as crows or ravens, that were scorching the Earth. Yi also shot several monsters, which had appeared in the terrible heat, leaving humankind forever grateful. (*See also* SUN, *p26.*)

A bow was a widely used symbol for males and manhood in China; hung by a door, it signified the birth of a son. The word for "young boy" (*zi*) is combined with that for "bow" to mean a musical bow (*gong zi*), the kind that would be used for an instrument such as the *erhu*, the Chinese two-stringed fiddle, or an instrument in the Western string family.

# RICE

**MI**

生米煮成熟饭
**"The rice has been cooked – what has been done cannot be undone."**

It has been suggested that the character for hulled rice (米 *mi*) originated as a pictograph of six rice grains being separated during the process of threshing. This later developed into an image of four rice grains, separated by a cross.

It was in China that rice, the staple food of East Asia and many other parts of the world, was first cultivated, certainly by around 7000BCE and perhaps even earlier. According to legend, it was Shen Nong, the Divine Farmer and one of the mythical first three rulers of China, who introduced the cultivation of this crucial and highly esteemed grain (*see also* FARMER, *p96*). By 1000BCE, complex

irrigation systems were already in place in the Yangzi valley to ensure sufficient water for rice paddies. These paddies are still a common sight today, and China is currently the largest producer of rice in the world.

An important component of daily life, rice has various symbolic connotations for the Chinese. Round, sweetened rice cakes are eaten at Chinese New Year as emblems of harmony and peace, while rice cakes with sweet and savoury fillings are among the traditional fare eaten two weeks later, on the first full moon of the year.

In addition to the multiple culinary uses of rice, the various

parts of the rice plant are employed in a wide range of ways, from fermenting liquor (into rice wine) to papermaking.

Rice is also traditionally regarded as one of the Twelve Ornaments, and "rice china" is a name given to porcelain decorated with small holes which are then glazed over, in imitation of rice. In the later imperial period, a disk covered in rice grains was one of the Twelve Symbols of Imperial Authority, representing the sovereign's ability to feed his people.

**RIGHT: 19th-century woodblock print of weeds being pulled up in a rice paddy field, as explained in the accompanying standard script inscription. The larger text at the top is in running script and praises the strength of the rice seedlings, describing how wonderful they look in the clear water.**

豊茜番翼翼
翠翠出清漣
溲茨稊
業業生可
菶日孔
種句應
莨苾雜虫
菶夜根
菶敗嘉
禾

一耘
時雨既已潤良
苗日維新去草
如去惡務令盡
陳根泥蟠任犢
鼻膝行生浪紋
睿惟有虞氏德
盛感鳥耘

# CERAMICS
## WA

宁为玉碎，不为瓦全

**"It is much better to be a broken piece
of jade than an intact piece of pottery."**

A pictograph showing the side view of semi-cylindrical roof tiles – with convex and concave sides alternating, and mortar to fix the join – lies behind the character 瓦 *wa*, which means "tile" and, by extension, "pottery" or "ceramics" in general.

The traditional curved shape of Chinese tiles may derive from the ancient use of sections of split bamboo in building, which were later reproduced in more durable earthenware. Tiles became a key feature of Chinese architecture, since the roof of a building was protective, decorative and also an indicator of social status. Initially plain, by the later Han dynasty tiles were being produced in a wide range of coloured glazes. The characteristic upturned eaves of Chinese roofs, sometimes adorned with ceramic figures of protective deities and beasts, are supposedly designed to propel evil spirits back up into the air, away from the building and its occupants.

This character is also used in various compound characters as a radical to indicate that their meaning is connected to pottery and ceramics, as, for example, in the character for *ci* (porcelain) – China's best-known invention. Porcelain is extremely hard pottery fired at very high temperatures, made principally from fine-grained *kaolin* or "china clay", which abounds in some areas of China. The exquisitely translucent, pure white porcelain for which China became famous in Europe and the Islamic world was perfected from the early 1300s under the Song, Yuan and Ming dynasties. However, a form of hard "proto-porcelain" was already being produced under the Shang dynasty nearly three millennia earlier. In the 17th and 18th centuries imported porcelain was known in English as "chinaware", because it came from China, and the title was later abbreviated simply to "china" – a name that stuck even after Europeans finally succeeded in producing their own version of porcelain.

**LEFT: Detail of an early Ming dynasty porcelain dish with a double phoenix design. Blue-and-white porcelain originated in China, as early as the 9th century CE. Designs such as this would have been painted with a cobalt-oxide pigment and then fired at a high temperature.**

# SILK
## SI

单丝不成线。

**"One strand of silk does not make a thread."**

The character for silk (絲 *si*) derives from a clear repeated image of strands of silk being twined into silk thread, the essence of which is still discernible in the current-day character.

This renowned fabric was first created in China, between 5000 and 3000BCE. Legend credits the wife of Huangdi, one of the Three Sovereigns, with its invention, and sericulture (silk farming) is one of China's most ancient and famous industries. *Si* was one of the first Chinese words to be adopted in a Western language – it is the source of the Latin *sericum*, the word from which "silk" itself derives. Indeed, the ancient Romans were among those who marvelled at this fabric, which is soft, lightweight, strong, durable, ideal for dyeing, cool in the heat and warm in the cold, with fibres so fine they can be used to embroider intricate patterns and motifs. These evocative textural associations mean that *si* is used in several compounds in Chinese, such as that for dark hair, *qing si*, literally "blue silk".

Silk was, and still is, a symbol of great wealth and luxury in China, associated with kings and emperors. From at least as early as the 5th century BCE there were workshops producing silk for the clothes and furnishings of the upper classes of society. There is also evidence of silk being exported to Russia and Germany during this period. In the 2nd century BCE the growing demand for silk among the élites of Europe, the Middle East and India gave rise to the famous Silk Road, the arduous overland trade routes westward from China, along which countless other Chinese inventions – from paper to gunpowder – were to travel to western Eurasia and the Indian subcontinent.

Silk production depends on the silkworm, a caterpillar fed on mulberry leaves that weaves a cocoon of silk thread around itself. Left to itself, the silkworm would eventually emerge from its cocoon as a moth, splitting the prized silk fibres. So, once the cocoons have been spun, they are immersed in boiling water and the cocoon is then carefully unravelled so that its strands can be spun into thread.

**RIGHT: Aristocrat's robe made from velvet with a dragon pattern picked out in multicoloured and gold-wrapped silk, dating from the 17th century.**

# LEATHER

**GE**

青山处处埋忠骨，何需马革裹尸还

**"A soldier's body can be buried in any green mountains;
it need not be returned home wrapped in a horse hide."**

The pictograph from which 革 *ge* evolved can be interpreted as two hands stripping the hide from a sheep or similar horned animal, its horns indicated by a horizontal stroke.

Although little leather survives from early times, the ancient Chinese were clearly skilled leatherworkers, particularly for equestrian and military use. Leather boots first appeared in the Chinese heartland in 325BCE when King Wuling of the state of Zhao equipped his troops with them, inspired by the nomadic tribesmen of the far north. However, linen and straw were still favoured for everyday footwear until durable leather shoes appeared around the time of the Han dynasty (206BCE–220CE). Several shoes discovered at Dunhuang in Gansu province in 2006 date to this era; made of pigskin and sheepskin, they are the oldest existing Chinese leather shoes.

The troops of the previous dynasty, the Qin (221–207BCE) had sported elaborate fish-scale armour of overlapping leather panels, worn by many of the soldiers in the First Emperor's Terracotta Army. His horses were also equipped with sophisticated leather harnesses, as seen on the model chariots also found in the emperor's tomb complex. The character for "saddle" (鞍 *an*) combines 革 *ge* with 安 *an* ("peace"). In this compound, 安 *an* not only indicates the pronunciation, but adds to the meaning, as it can also mean "safety". Similarly, the character for "brake" (勒 *le*) is represented by a compound of *ge* and 力 *li* meaning "strength", originally a reference to reining in an animal.

Because of the process of stripping the flesh and hair off a hide, this character is also used to convey the sense of "eliminate" and "transform". *Ge* in this sense combined with *ming* ("order" or "command", and also "life" and "destiny") produces *ge ming*, meaning "revolution" in the political sense, and *ge* also occurs in other terms relating to reform. *Ge zhi* means "demote" or "remove" from "office" (*zhi*) – rather like the English phrase "to be stripped of office".

# METAL

## JIN

金无足赤，人无完人
**"No piece of gold is one hundred per cent pure,
just as no man is perfect."**

In the epigraphic form of the character 金 *jin*, meaning "metal", there are two dots that represent lumps of ores at the left-hand side. At the right-hand side is a combination of an arrow-head, made of metal, and the radical for "soil" or "earth" (土), to indicate that ores for producing metals are found in the ground. In the seal script, the ores were moved into the spaces around the "earth" radical and the arrow-head was pushed upward, forming the basis for the present-day character. In contemporary Chinese the word *jin* is most often used to denote "gold".

According to the theory of the Five Phases of ancient Chinese philosophy, metal corresponds to the colour white, the direction west, the season autumn, the planet Venus and the organ lung.

In ancient China, for more than 1,000 years the most important metal was bronze. Casting bronze required relatively complex technology, and because of the high cost of labour involved in their production, exquisitely manufactured bronze vessels symbolized their owner's wealth and power. Bronze vessels for food and wine played a crucial part in sacred ceremonies, and their size and number in a ruler's collection became the absolute status symbol in the inter-tribal political arena.

The smelting and casting of metals in pre-modern times was essentially a trial-and-error process. A widespread legend tells of how an official was in charge of a smelting process that began to go wrong because the temperature in the furnace was not right. In order to save him from the capital punishment he might face as a result, his wife threw herself into the furnace to ensure the success of the metal extraction.

# JADE

**YU**

玉不琢，不成器

**"Jade cannot be made into a piece of jewelry or a curio without being chiselled and worked upon."**

Oracle bone versions of the character 玉 *yu* for "jade" look like a cluster of several jade pieces strung together, a common way to display this precious stone as an ornament. Later, in its seal script form, the cluster was reduced to three horizontal lines, resulting in virtually the same form as the character for "king" (王). In order to distinguish the two, a dot was added to the character for "jade".

While a large proportion of ancient *yu* pieces are nephrites (the hard, pale green stone that we associate with jade), in Chinese the word *yu* is, in fact, a cultural concept rather than a homogenously physical one, and means "precious stone". Many other minerals were also considered to be *yu*. In ancient times, *yu* was made into ornaments such as pendants and earrings; however, carved *yu* objects of spiritual and political significance were the most highly valued. These objects were used in rituals to communicate with deities and for ancestor worship, and were buried with deceased rulers of the community.

Confucius once summarized five human virtues that he saw embodied in *yu*: humanity is represented in its warm glow; moral integrity in its purity; wisdom in its pleasant ringing sound; justice in its hardness; perseverance in its durability. This observation added much to jade's value and symbolism.

The Chinese adored jade so much that they invented hundreds of characters that contain the radical 玉 *yu* and describe positive qualities such as beauty, power and value, as well as numerous different types of *yu* and its products. *Yu* is also used as a positive intensifier for other words – for example, "gourmet food" is *yu shi*, "beautiful women", *yu nu*, and the supreme god in the heavens, *yu huang*.

RIGHT: Qing dynasty jade box in the shape of eight geese amongst leaves (ca. 1750–1820). Carved from a single piece of jade, this intricate piece is divided horizontally, with the body of each goose hollowed out to form a small container.

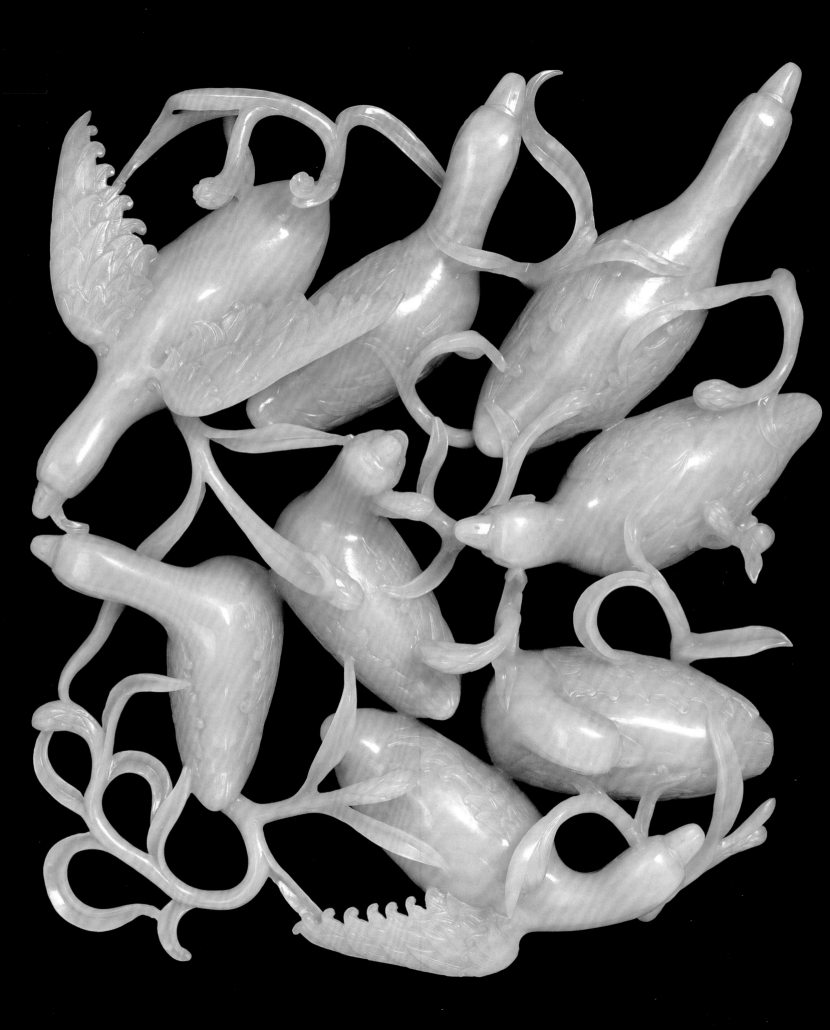

# PAPER

## ZHI

纸包不住火
**"One cannot wrap fire in paper."**

The history of Chinese writing surfaces is encapsulated in the character for "paper", 紙 *zhi*, a compound of the radical for "silk" (*see p134*) plus that for "plant roots" (*shi*) as a phonetic guide.

Paper is one of the Four Great Inventions of Ancient China (a term coined by Western scholars), the others being printing, the compass and gunpowder. It is also one of the Four Treasures of the Scholar's Study (*see also* PEN, *p144*). Few inventions have had greater impact on the world in terms of the arts, culture, communication and the spread of ideas. Paper also greatly facilitated the development of woodblock printing, which was being practised in China several centuries before Johannes Gutenberg in Europe.

As their written language developed, the Chinese used a variety of surfaces to write on, including tortoise shells, ox shoulderblades and pottery. Strips of wood or bamboo were also used, joined lengthways into rather cumbersome rolls, and were common and cheap. Their use probably explains why Chinese was almost exclusively written in vertical columns until relatively recently. As the character for *zhi* suggests, silk was used, too – it was easy to write on with a brush, but for most practical purposes prohibitively expensive.

The first attempts to make paper probably took place during the early Han dynasty (206BCE–220CE), the process involved shredding old rags to fibres, mixing the fibres with water, then using a mould to hold the fibres as the water drained off. The water expanded the fibres, which then bound together as they dried to form a sheet.

Once the basic technique had appeared, the Chinese experimented with a range of raw materials to make paper. Mulberry bark, rattan, bamboo and stalks of rice and wheat all provided suitable fibres. In the workshops of Emperor He Di (ruled 88–106CE), an imperial eunuch, Cai Lun (ca. 50–121CE), achieved fame by manufacturing a paper of greatly improved quality, using a combination of materials such as bark, silk, hemp and fishing net. From this time on paper became the most widely used writing surface in China.

**FOLLOWING PAGES: Strips of Chinese calligraphy hanging up to dry. All of the pieces are in clerical script and reproduce ancient didactic texts apart from the one hanging second from the left, which is a Tang dynasty poem in running script.**

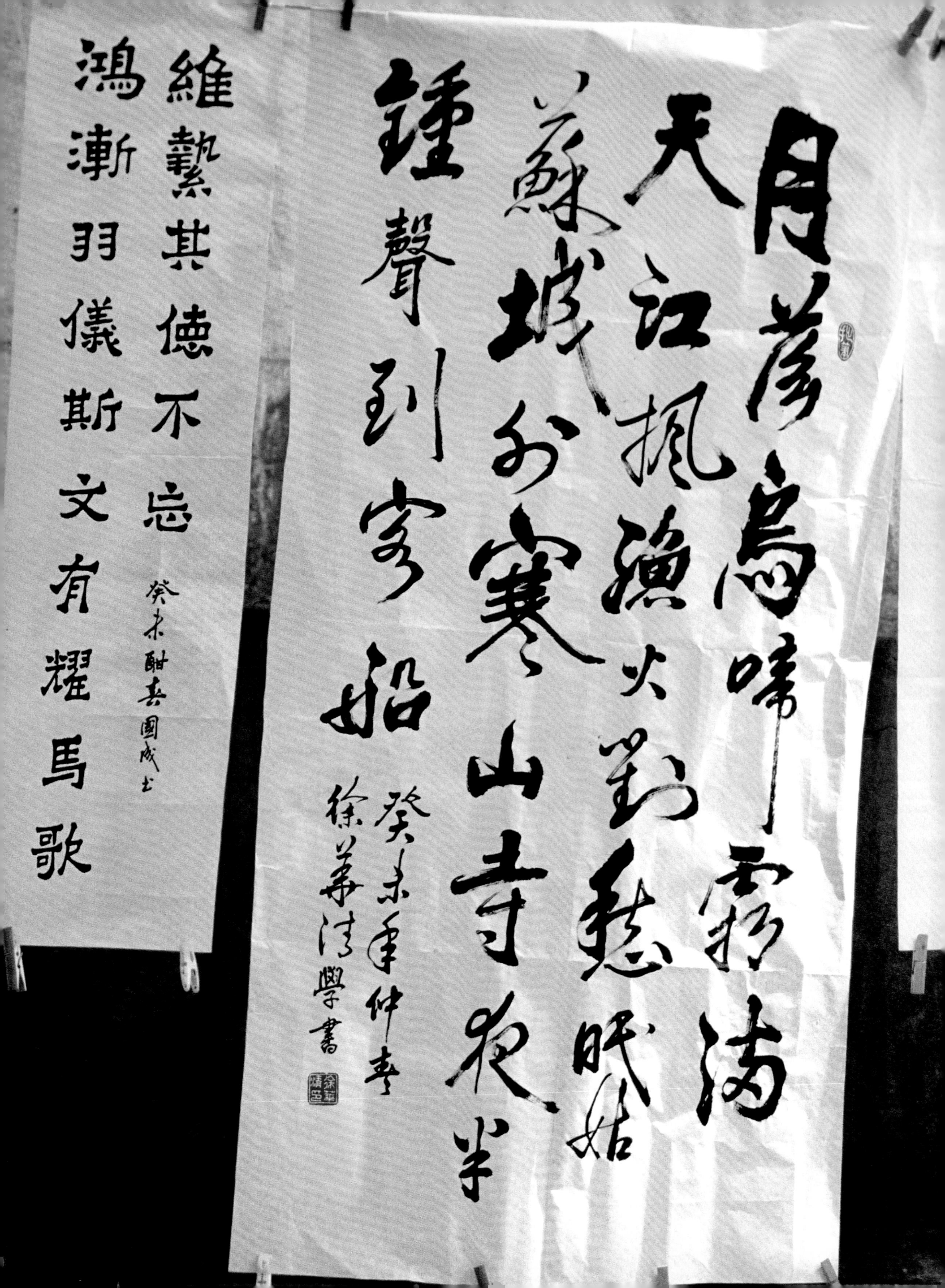

維鸑其德不忘
鴻漸羽儀斯文有耀鳴歌

癸未酬春園成士

月落烏啼霜滿天，江楓漁火對愁眠。姑蘇城外寒山寺，夜半鐘聲到客船。

癸未重陽仲秋 徐華清學書

與時俱進

共鑄輝煌

廣州市嶺海老人大學二十周年紀念

以示省老人保健大學敬賀

行葦歌仁廿棠詠德潛龍

# PEN

**BI**

好记性不如烂笔头

**"The palest ink is better than the best memory."**

The character 筆 *bi*, which means "pen" or "writing implement", is a compound of the radical for "bamboo" above that for "writing brush" (*yu*), which originally depicted a hand holding a pen. The addition of bamboo indicates the bamboo-handled writing brush that until recently was the usual Chinese writing implement.

This type of brush was in use in prehistoric China and may even predate the written language – designs on Neolithic pottery were clearly made with a sort of brush and some characters on oracle bones of the Shang dynasty (ca. 1500–ca. 1050BCE) were written in vermilion ink with a brush before being engraved. In later periods, luxury pens sometimes had handles made of other materials, such as porcelain. The earliest surviving brush dates from the Warring States period (453–221BCE), and has a bamboo handle and a rabbit-hair tip.

The soft, flexible tip of the *bi* that lends itself to flowing expressive strokes has played a large part in the development of Chinese calligraphy. Control of the brush is its chief discipline, determining the strength, width and direction of each stroke. The brush is held vertically, but there are no strict rules as to which fingers to use. From the 3rd century onward, calligraphy came to be viewed as an art form in itself, and a sign of personal cultivation for all *literati*. These included China's most famous master of the pen, Wang Xizhi (303–361CE), who is known as the "sacred calligrapher". A brush or "brush-pen" is, therefore, one of the Four Treasures of the Scholar's Study along with paper, ink and ink stone.

Today, brushes used for calligraphy and painting usually have a bamboo handle, although sandalwood, jade, silver and other materials are sometimes used for more precious brushes. Usually indicated on the handle is the type of hair, or combination of hairs, that the brush is made from, such as goat, hare or wolf – each of which has particular qualities of texture, absorbency and resilience.

# CLASSICS

**DIAN**

典籍礼度，无心於治，而所以为治
"Classics and rites were not created with the aim of governance, yet that is why they are the most effective tools for governance."

"Books placed on a pedestal" is both the literal and figurative meaning of the character 典 *dian*. Early epigraphic forms show an ancient book made of bound strips of bamboo or wood (*see* PAPER, *p140*) set on a pedestal or prop (*ji*) out of reverence. The epigraphic form shown here also includes what is probably a hand reaching for the book on its stand.

The term "classics" in China essentially refers to the Confucian canon – books that form the basis of traditional Confucian ethics, practice and philosophical enquiry. Confucians have drawn lessons from these books for centuries – for appropriate living in general and moral government in particular. As the core texts for the imperial civil service examinations from 1313 to 1905, the classics were once memorized by every aspiring scholar, and many phrases and sayings from them have entered everyday Chinese speech.

The content of the canon has varied over time, but at its heart are what are known as the Five Classics and the Four Books. The Five Classics were the works that Confucius (551–479BCE) himself employed to teach with: the *Classic of Changes* (*Yi Jing* or *I Ching*), the *Classic of Documents* (*Shu Jing*), the *Classic of Poetry* (*Shi Jing*), the *Record of Ritual* (*Li Ji*) and the *Spring and Autumn Annals* (*Chunqiu*). A sixth classic, the *Classic of Music* (*Yue Jing*), was lost before 200BCE. The Four Books, assembled more than 1,000 years later by the scholar Zhu Xi (1130–1200), are thought to sum up Confucius's teachings. They are the *Analects* (*Lunyu*), Confucius's sayings and conversations; the *Mencius* (*Mengzi*), the writings of his great follower of that name; the *Great Learning* (*Daxue*), which teaches the cultivation of morals; and the *Doctrine of the Mean* (*Zhongyong*), which expresses the idea that humans and the cosmos form a unified whole.

# MAP

**TU**

图穷匕首见

"A map was presented to the First Emperor. When it was unrolled, a dagger that was to be used to assassinate him was discovered hidden there – a concealed intention finally made known."

The line around the edge of the epigraphic form of the character 圖 *tu*, meaning "map", is supposed to represent the territory of a state or country and it encloses a radical (啚) that means "rural settlements", clearly conveying the primary function of the earliest maps.

Maps undoubtedly served a practical purpose in ancient China, particularly in relation to military manoeuvres and defence. China's oldest extant true maps were found in 1986. They had been buried with a military officer of the Qin kingdom who died in around 239BCE in his tomb at Fangmatan, Gansu province. The seven maps are each drawn to scale in ink on four wooden boards and depict the ancient county of Guixian. They show towns, army camps, rivers, mountain passes, forests and checkpoints. Like many traditional Chinese maps they are oriented with south, the prime cardinal direction, at the top (*see* SOUTH, *p165*).

Maps were also drawn for royal use in ancient China. The earliest Chinese reference to a map is a bronze inscription of the Zhou period, which describes King Kang (1005–978BCE) examining the maps of his predecessors, King Wu and Cheng, before setting out on a royal procession. Bronze inscriptions from later in the dynasty refer to other types of map as well, and indicate that there was a map chamber in the royal palace.

Western-style maps arrived in China with the Jesuit missionaries of the 16th and 17th centuries. There was long resistance to European cartography, partly because Western maps were oriented with north at the top, but also because they did not place China at the centre of the world. Modern Chinese maps follow international conventions. However, directions such as "northwest" and "southeast" continue to be expressed in Chinese as "westnorth", "eastsouth" and so on.

# PAINTING
## HUA

画龙画虎难画骨，
知人知面不知心

**"When drawing a dragon or a tiger, you can only draw their appearance but not their bones; when getting acquainted with a person, you may only know his face but not his true nature."**

The ancient pictograph for "painting" represents a hand wielding a brush over a piece of paper or perhaps a stretched frame of silk. Though stylized, this image remains little changed in the modern-day character.

Traditional painting in China is learnt in the same way as calligraphy, with a brush and ink. The two art forms are closely interlinked and have been highly revered in China for centuries – the Ming dynasty scholar Li Rihua (1565–1635) ranked painting and calligraphy as the most prestigious of all art forms. Painting was a favourite occupation of the *literati*, or gentlemen scholar-officials (see SCHOLAR, *p94*), whose Confucian education included mastering the skill of using a calligraphy brush. A gentleman artist such as Ni Zan (1301–1374), one of the Four Great Masters of the Yuan, might combine the two disciplines, painting a landscape and then inscribing it in fine calligraphy, with a poem of his own composition.

For Ni Zan and others, the chief aesthetic ideal was *pingdan*, or "unadorned elegance". In traditional landscape paintings, elements are therefore often described in muted colours or, especially in the rendering of water, left blank, so that the paper shows through. Also, unlike much Western art, they often lack a fixed centre of perspective. Such paintings are not intended to give an accurate account of a scene, rather convey a particular mood or quality.

Chinese art, particularly as patronized by the imperial court, reflected Confucian notions that society might be positively influenced by the contemplation of the order of nature in all its splendour. Virtually every motif also had a symbolic significance, derived from the Chinese classics. Plants such as bamboo, pines and plum blossom (see *pp64–75*) each represented admirable human qualities, while a solitary figure in an ethereal and exquisitely rendered landscape might convey an aloofness from worldly attachments. These symbols were often used to convey auspicious and congratulatory messages and at times, for example under the Yuan (Mongol) dynasty (1279–1368), conveyed a sense of integrity and endurance under uncongenial foreign regimes.

Like the many other Chinese arts, painting did not develop in isolation, of course, nor was it unevolving. Over the centuries Chinese painting absorbed influences from cultures as diverse as Tibet, Iran and, from the Qing dynasty onward, Europe.

# ZITHER
## QIN

对牛弹琴
**"A cow cannot appreciate the subtlety of zither-playing."**

The character 琴 *qin* derives from a simplified depiction of the *qin* itself – a plucked seven-stringed instrument of the zither family (sometimes, less accurately, translated as a "lute"). The traditional *qin* is often referred to today as the *guqin* ("ancient qin") or *qixianqin* (seven-stringed qin) to distinguish it from other stringed instruments now encompassed by the generic term *qin*.

The ancient *qin* is the most venerable of the Chinese stringed instruments, and its invention is traditionally ascribed to the god Fuxi, the first of the Three Sovereigns, China's primordial first rulers, who is said to have ruled 5,000 years ago.

The *qin*'s slender body is 130cm (51in) long, 20cm (8in) wide and 5cm (2in) thick, and is made of wood – ideally of straight-grained paulownia or China fir (a variety of cypress) for the upper part, and catalpa for the base, which has two holes (known as the "phoenix pool" and the "dragon pond") to release the sound. The seven strings are stretched along the upper face of the instrument, which also bears thirteen inlaid jade markers. A *qin* player lays the instrument on a horizontal surface such as a table and then plucks the strings to make the sound.

The Four Arts of a Scholar, the accomplishments that are supposed to demonstrate a person's education and true breeding, are music, chess, painting and calligraphy, usually represented in art respectively by a *qin*, a chessboard, a painting scroll and a person holding a brush-pen.

The word is a homophone of *qin* meaning "prohibit", and it was once explained that the rich tones of the instrument – by turns ethereal and robust – could exclude all evil and negative feelings. The *qin* has a larger companion, the *se*, and two zithers together symbolize marital bliss, which is expressed in Chinese by the phrase *qin se he ming* – "the *qin* and the *se* singing in harmony".

性質

QUALITIES

| 陰 | 陽 | 黑 | 白 | 赤 |
|---|---|---|---|---|
| 青 | 黃 | 北 | 南 | 東 |
| 西 | 中 | 福 | 愛 | 情 |
| 壽 | 安 | 孝 | 信 | 忠 |
| 美 | 貴 | | | |

万物负阴而抱阳

**"Every living thing turns to the sun (yang) and away from the shade (yin)."**

## YIN

The character 陰 yin literally means "shady", although it has come to signify a far more complex and wide-ranging concept. The epigraphic form of this character indicated the northern, shaded side of a valley, deriving from a depiction of a hill or mountain – interpreted as a slope with horizontal agricultural terraces – followed by a pictograph that represents "clouded".

In traditional Chinese cosmology, the yin and yang are the opposing but necessarily coexisting forces that give rise to all the phenomena of the universe. The two words have come to embrace a wide range of complementary pairs, such

as darkness (yin) and light (yang), although it is always understood that these are not mutually exclusive opposites but polarities that balance each other, with gradation and constant interaction between them. This is reflected in the familiar form of the taiji, the "supreme ultimate", the popular round emblem that shows the yin and yang flowing into one another, and each containing the seed of the other.

Yin came to represent qualities such as passivity, receptivity, yielding, femininity, darkness, coldness, heaviness, quiet, tranquillity and moisture. It also represents the Earth, which is said to have coagulated

from pure yin at the beginning of time. It is associated with low-lying geographical features such as valleys and streams. The moon and night-time are yin, and yin energy reaches its peak at the winter solstice, the darkest and least active point in nature's annual cycle. Each of the eight trigrams (ba gua) set out in the Yi Jing (I Ching), or Book of Changes, the classic Chinese work of divination, consists of three lines – either broken ones representing yin or unbroken ones representing yang, in various orders and combinations. The trigram of three broken lines stands for pure yin.

立天之道，曰阴与阳

**"The fundamental way of the universe
is the interaction between *yin* and *yang*."**

# YANG

The literal meaning of 陽 *yang* is "sunny", and the character originally denoted the southern, sunny side of a mountain, comprising of the element "mountain" or "hill", which also occurs in *yin*, followed by a representation of the sun rising above the horizon and shining forth its rays.

This imagery of the hillsides is strikingly apt in this pair of characters, *yin* and *yang*: just as the border between the sunny and shady areas is unfixed as the sun moves across the sky, so the boundary between the forces of *yin* and *yang* is in a permanent state of flux. *Yang* is said to have arisen first in the world, and to be the proactive, leading force of

the two. However, it cannot exist alone, and *yin* is never entirely overwhelmed, just as the north slope of a hillside will never be in full sunlight, and sometimes, just as the south slope will be almost entirely in darkness at night, *yang* must yield to *yin*. Moreover, the brighter the light, the stronger the shadows.

As the concept of *yang* developed in ancient China, it came to represent qualities such as activity, penetration, domination, masculinity, light, heat, lightness, noise, vigour and dryness. It represents Heaven, and is therefore associated with elevated geographical features such as mountains. Its symbol is the dragon, the greatest of

celestial creatures. The sun and daytime are *yang*, and *yang* energy reaches its peak at the summer solstice, the brightest point in nature's annual cycle. In the *Yi Jing* (*I Ching*), the trigram of three solid lines stands for pure *yang* (*see opposite*).

# BLACK

## HEI

天下乌鸦一般黑
**"All crows under the sun are black."**

The early forms of the character 黑 *hei* meaning "black" have been interpreted as a radical showing two fires (炎) to denote "fierce fire", underneath an image of what is probably a fire duct enclosing dots of black soot.

Black is the colour of the north and winter. It also represents the element water, and hence roof tiles in China are often black, as a symbolic protection from the rain. Black is also associated with the Black Tortoise, one of China's Four Celestial Creatures, after whom a constellation is named. When, late in the year, this constellation appears to rise in the northeast and set in the northwest, it traditionally marks winter's onset. In its animal form, the Black Tortoise is sometimes depicted entwined with a snake, and together they are known as the Black Warrior.

Black has both negative and positive associations in China. It is linked closely with death, and the Chinese black crow (*wuya*) is a bird of ill omen. However, black birds are not always associated with bad luck. A painting of a crow (*ya*) with six persimmons (*shi*) plays on the homophonous phrase *ya shi*, meaning "elegant gentleman-scholar". A black ox is often connected to the philosopher Laozi, the legendary founder of Daoism, who is said to have gone into exile in the west riding on such a creature. Black can also signify honour – in Chinese theatre, black-faced figures will usually be rough diamonds, coarse and unrefined but also honest.

The traditional colour of Chinese calligraphy ink is black, too, and so the characters for "black" and "earth" combine to give the character for "ink" (*mo*), which is traditionally obtained by grinding ink "cake" (soot mixed with a kind of glue and allowed to solidify) on an ink stone with water.

**RIGHT: Four seal script characters,**
*tian fu yong cang* ("eternal collection of the heavenly palace"), carved into an ink cake, attributed to Wang Weigao, Qing dynasty, 19th century.

# WHITE

**BAI**

白圭之玷，尚可磨也；斯言之玷，不可为也
**"A blemish on a piece of white jade may be ground away with patience; but what can be done for a mistake made in a speech? It is beyond our reach."**

There are several different interpretations of the formation of the character 白 *bai* meaning "white". According to some scholars, the earliest form denotes a brilliant, sharp ray of light beaming out of the top of the sun during sunrise, which would turn the sky around it white. Others regard the shape as that of a grain of white rice. Yet another explanation is that the shape is a thumb, which was a character meaning "first", and was borrowed to mean "white" because the two spoken words share the same pronunciation.

White is associated with the element metal and with the White Tiger constellation, which appears to set with the sun in the western sky. It is also connected with the season autumn, and therefore with advancing age.

As in the West, white has connotations of purity in China, and a virgin is sometimes described as *qing bai*, or "pure white". Traditionally, the rare sighting of a white-haired animal, such as a deer or an ape, was considered auspicious, and a good omen for the emperor's governance. However, white also has several negative connotations. In Chinese theatre, white-faced men are sly and untrustworthy, unlike the honest black-faced characters (*see p154*). It is unlucky to wear a white flower or any other white object in your hair, and after a death a white cloth is traditionally hung over the doorway. However, it is not strictly true that white is the principal colour of mourning in China. During mourning, some relatives of the deceased might wear unbleached sackcloth hoods of a pale oatmeal colour, but the main mourning clothes are dark for the nearest kin (children and daughters-in-law) and progressively lighter for grandchildren and great-grandchildren. Only outsiders, such as sons-in-law, who belong to a different household, will wear mainly white clothes.

# RED

## CHI

近墨者黑，近朱者赤

**"If you are too close to vermilion dye, you will be stained red;
if you are too close to ink, you will be stained black."**

Red is literally the "colour of great flames", and the character 赤 *chi* therefore combines the radical for "large" – a star-like form of a man standing with legs set wide and arms outstretched – above that for "fire".

Red is the first of the Five Colours of Chinese Cosmology (the others being white, blue, yellow and black), and the colour of the south, summer and the element fire. It is represented in the night sky by the Red Bird constellation.

The most auspicious of all colours, red also symbolizes light, Heaven, the sun, gold and prosperity. It is the hue that most embodies the dynamism of *yang* (*see p153*), and is traditionally believed to have magical powers that can drive off demons. In the Qing dynasty (1644–1911), emperors and their officials wore predominantly dark blue robes, rejecting the traditional red of their Ming predecessors; but even a Qing ruler was obliged to wear auspicious red for the crucial imperial sacrifices at the Altar of the Sun in Beijing.

The positive associations of red are still widely emphasized in China today. On the stock market boards the figures going up are coloured red, and as the colour of celebration and festivity par excellence, red is especially prominent at Chinese New Year and many other festivals. At traditional weddings, the bride will wear red, guests will offer the couple gifts of money inside little red envelopes, and the character for "happiness" or "joy" (*xi*) will be almost everywhere, either in red characters or in gold on a red background. The association is also expressed in language – commenting that someone has a "red gall-bladder" (*chi dan*) or a "red heart" (*hong xin*) in Chinese means that that person is loyal.

In the 19th century, Western socialists adopted the red flag – in Europe, an old banner of warning and defiance – as the emblem of international revolution. This was a gift to Chinese communists, who effectively exploited the colour's traditional symbolism for their own purposes.

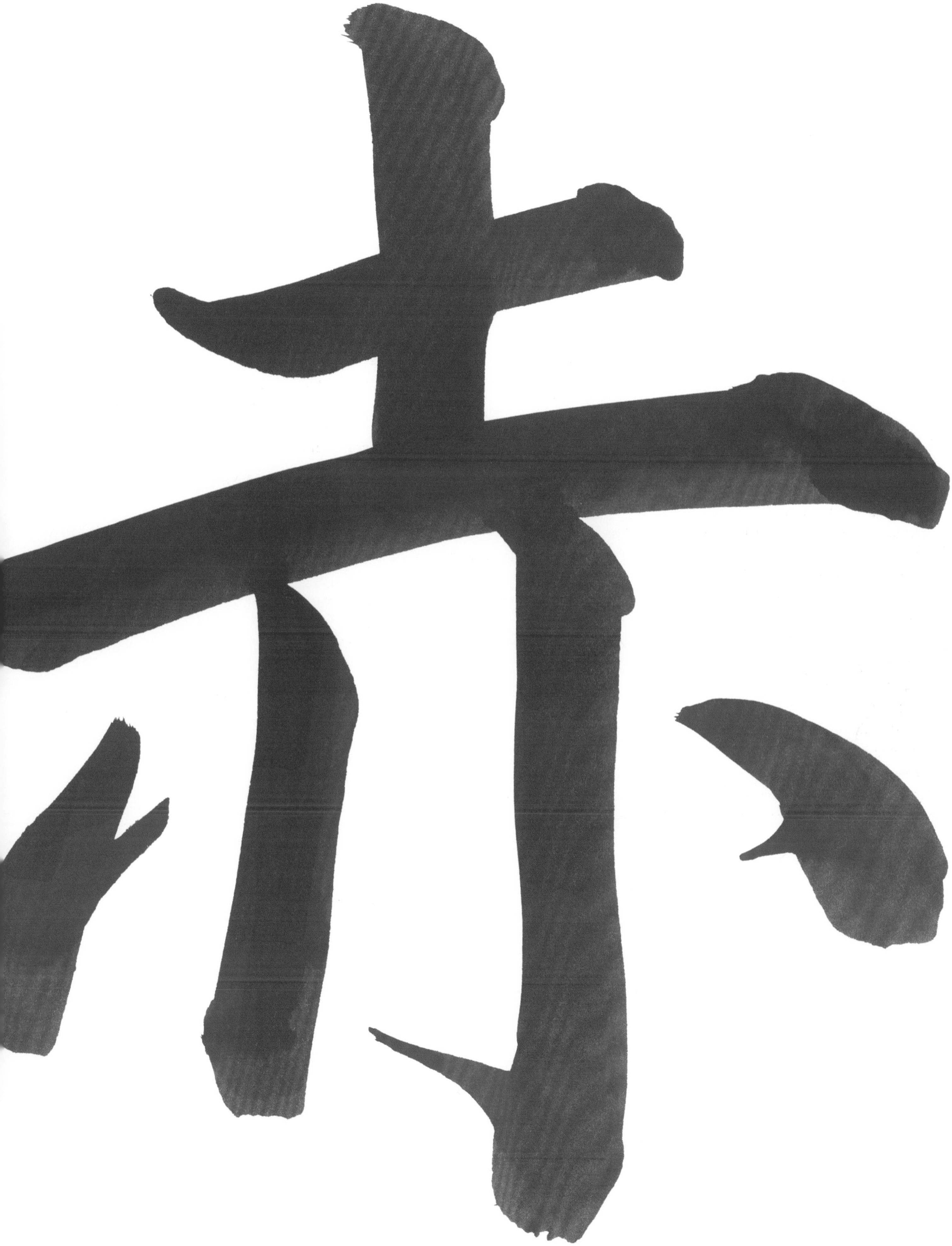

# BLUE

## QING

青出于蓝而胜于蓝
**"Blue pigment comes from the indigo plant, but is bluer than the plant itself."**

The meaning of the character 青 *qing* actually embraces a wide range of colours, including what Westerners would call green, and the inky grey of a thundercloud, as well as all shades of blue. Not a great deal is known about its formation. However, one recent view is that the top part of the epigraphic form of this character is related to grass and therefore indicates the "colour of grass or plants"; and that the lower part is an image of a mine pit, perhaps symbolizing an ore that is a green-blue colour.

The Blue (or Green) Dragon is one of the most ancient creatures of Chinese mythology. It appears in the eastern night sky as a constellation, which in ancient times was visible above China from March onward. For this reason the dragon and the colour blue/green became associated with spring and the east. One of the Five Colours of Chinese Cosmology, *qing* is also linked with the element wood.

The word *qing* sounds the same as *qing*, meaning "pure" or "honest", which was adopted by China's last imperial rulers, the Manchu, as their dynastic name. The Qing (1644–1911) also adopted a navy-blue or indigo surcoat as the "uniform" of their regime, in reference to their name and in deliberate contrast to the red of the dynasty they had ousted, the Ming (whose name means literally "brightness"). From the reign of the Emperor Yongzheng (1723–1735) onward, blue-and-white Qing vases featuring prominent lotus motifs were often given as awards to certain officials by the emperor, since "blue lotus" (*qing lian*) is a homophone of "honest" (*qing*) and "virtuous" (*lian*).

For emperors throughout the dynasties, dark blue was the correct colour to wear for the annual imperial rites at the Altar of Heaven, and light blue at the Altar of the Moon.

**FOLLOWING PAGES, LEFT:** Qing dynasty silk robe in shades of blue and white.
**RIGHT:** Detail of a Chinese temple roof.

# YELLOW

## HUANG

三人一条心，黄土变成金
**"Three men with one mind can turn yellow earth into gold."**

The oldest character for 黄 *huang* combines the radicals for "colour" and "fields". The reference to fields derives from the yellow loess deposits that blow across China's northern plains from the Gobi Desert, or are laid down as rich silt by the spring floods of the Yellow River (Huang He), giving the river its name. Indeed, the phrase "Yellow Earth" is a common metaphor for "China".

Among the Five Colours, yellow is the representative of the centre (*see also* MIDDLE, *p168*) and of the element earth. As a symbol of the land they ruled, yellow was therefore a symbolic colour for the Chinese emperors, who wore formal court robes of yellow, and also special yellow robes when performing the yearly rites at the Altar of the Earth in Beijing.

According to Chinese myth, these and other annual imperial sacrifices to the sun, moon and to Heaven were instituted by the legendary emperor, Huangdi (the "Yellow Emperor", believed to have ruled 2697–2597BCE). Huangdi is credited with introducing warfare and defeating "barbarians" to establish the Chinese homeland in the plains of the Yellow River. His hundred-year reign is also said to have witnessed the invention of wooden houses, silk, boats, carts, ceramics, Chinese characters and the sixty-year Chinese calendar cycle. Huangdi is viewed as the "Father of Medicine", and much of the *Huangdi Neijing* (*The Yellow Emperor's Inner Canon*), a classic collection of medical works, is composed as a dialogue between Huangdi and his minister Qibo.

Yellow often has negative associations in the West (for example, it is associated with cowardice), but in China it is a highly auspicious colour. For example, a virgin is sometimes called a "yellow blossom", and yellow is also evocative of gold and prosperity.

# NORTH

**BEI**

南辕北辙

**"It is hard for you to go to your destination in the south by driving your chariot northward."**

In ancient China it was customary for people to sit facing the south toward the sun, with their backs to the north. So a pictograph of two figures back to back, facing opposite directions, conveyed the idea of "back", which also implied "north". The same character (北) also means "disagree" and "to flee after defeat", much like the English phrase "to turn one's back" on something.

One of the Five Directions of Chinese Cosmology (north, south, east, west and centre), north is associated with winter, rain and the colour black, and is symbolized by the celestial Black Tortoise and the Black Warrior (*see also* BLACK, *p154*).

Perhaps the traditional Chinese view of northerners as calmer, less excitable and more reliable than their compatriots in the hotter south has something to do with the fact that the North China Plain, traversed by the Yellow River, is the historical heartland of the Chinese state. It was from the north that most of China's mightiest rulers governed, from great capitals such as Chang'An (Xi'an), Kaifeng, Luoyang and Peking (Beijing).

The famous Great Wall of China was erected, and periodically rebuilt, to secure China's northern frontiers. Beyond them, for much of Chinese history, lay the threat of nomadic warrior peoples such as the Huns, Turks, Jurchen, Mongols and Manchu, who ranged the plains of central and northern Asia and viewed China as a rich prize.

When the Mongols seized control of China and established the Yuan dynasty (1279–1368), they ruled from a new city that they called Dadu, north of an earlier capital that had stood nearby. The Ming, who ousted the Yuan, were initially based further south in Nanjing, southern (*nan*) capital (*jing*), but moved to Dadu, renaming it Beijing, northern (*bei*) capital (*jing*). With brief intervals, Beijing has remained China's capital ever since.

# SOUTH

## NAN

寿比南山。

**"May you live as long as the southern mountains."**

The earliest version of the character 南 *nan* for "south" has been interpreted as a combination of two elements, meaning "vegetation" and "everywhere", referring to the increasingly subtropical character of the landscape as one travels south from the North China Plain toward the Yangzi and Pearl Rivers.

Symbolizing summer, the sun, the colour red and the element fire, south is the primary direction in Chinese cosmology, represented celestially as the Red Bird, which appears as a constellation in the southern night sky in late spring and summer (*see also* RED, *p158*). It was also once customary for the emperor to sit facing the south, while his courtiers faced the north.

As the most important cardinal direction, south was placed at the top of maps in China, before the adoption of European-style cartography from the 16th and 17th centuries (*see also* MAP, *p147*). Chinese cities were generally laid out along a central north-south axis, with temples, palaces and other important buildings all constructed facing the south along the main axis, and subsidiary buildings to either side.

As the domain of the sun, the south is also linked with Heaven (*tian*). Thus, the Forbidden City, the old imperial palace complex in Beijing (*see also* PALACE, *p124*), is entered from the south by the *Tiananmen*, the Gate of Heavenly Peace, while the Altar of Heaven, the scene of annual sacrifices made by the emperor, lies in the south of the old city. Nanjing, the "southern capital", was the seat of several Chinese dynasties and also of the Republic of China (founded in 1912) until the expulsion of its government to Taiwan in 1949.

Associated with the south is the fire god Zhu Rong, the Lord of the Southern Quarter, whose image, with its fiery red face, is still occasionally found on village doorposts to ward off accidental fires. The mountain ranges of southern China are associated with longevity, and traditional gifts for an elderly person's birthday will often be accompanied by the wish: "May you live as long as the southern mountains."

# EAST

**DONG**

东方不亮西方亮
**"When it is dark in the east, it must be bright in the west."**

The character 東 *dong* began as a simple representation of the sun rising behind a tree, perhaps an allusion to the myth that the sun lived in a giant celestial tree beyond the eastern horizon, from which it rose each morning and to which it returned each evening after setting in the west. In the myth of Yi the Archer, the tree is called the Fu Sang tree and was originally the home of ten suns (*see also* SUN *and* BOW, *pp26 and 129*).

As well as with the rising sun, the east is associated with the colour *qing* (*see* BLUE, *p160*), eternal life and the dynamic force of *yang*. Among the Five Elements it represents wood, and is represented by the celestial Blue (or Green) Dragon constellation, which appeared in the night sky from March onward in ancient times. The east is, therefore, also linked to this time of the year, spring – the season of nature's most vigorous growth and renewal, when the life-force is at its most potent.

It is toward the east that the three greatest rivers of China – the Yellow, the Yangzi and the Pearl – all flow, emptying into the seas that form China's eastern frontier.

Xi Wang Mu, the Queen Mother of the West (*see opposite*), is sometimes depicted with a male consort and counterpart named Dong Wang Gong, the King Father of the East, who is a minor figure in the later Chinese pantheon.

# WEST

## XI

不是东风压倒西风，就是西风压倒东风

**"If the east wind doesn't prevail over the west wind, then the west wind is bound to prevail over the east wind."**

Early forms of the character 西 *xi* for "west" have been interpreted to be the image of a bird roosting in its nest, which would have conveyed the idea of "sunset" – the time when birds go to roost – and, by extension, its direction, west.

The west is connected with the declining sun, both in terms of day turning into night and the changes that come with the autumn season. It is symbolically represented by the celestial White Tiger (*see also* WHITE, *p156*).

The popular Daoist goddess Xi Wang Mu, the Queen Mother of the West, is said to reside in the great Kunlun mountains, the abode of the celestial immortals far to the west of the ancient Chinese heartlands. Originally a fearsome deity, Xi Wang Mu later became the queen of Heaven. Frequently depicted in art, she was supposed to be the keeper of the elixir of eternal life, and the gods and goddesses replenished their immortality by eating the peaches that grew in her gardens.

Laozi, the legendary founder of Daoism, is said to have ridden into the west on an ox, and the west is also revered as the direction from which Buddhism travelled from India to China. The novel *Journey to the West*, by Wu Cheng'en (ca. 1500–ca. 1582), is a picaresque account of a famous real journey undertaken by the 7th-century monk Xuanzang, who went overland to India to collect Buddhist scriptures. Pure Land, a popular school of Buddhism in China and Japan, is named for the Western Paradise where those who invoked the name of Emituo (Amitabha in Sanskrit), a celestial form of the Buddha, would be reborn and cleansed of sin before attaining enlightenment.

The combination of the Chinese words for "east" and "west", *dong xi*, originally meant "from all over the world" and then later came to mean "things made all over the world". Today, *dong xi* has become a more generic term, equivalent to "anything", "everything" and "thing".

# MIDDLE

**ZHONG**

日中则昃
**"When the sun reaches its zenith, it is time for it to go down."**

An arrow piercing the centre of a target is the usual interpretation of the character 中 *zhong* meaning "middle" or "centre", and the same character is present in other composite characters such as those for "to strike" (a target) and "to hit the mark"; it also occurs in the verb *zhongcai*, "to win a prize in the lottery".

In China, the middle is considered to be the fifth "direction" uniting the four cardinal points of east, west, south and north. This five-point system corresponds to the crucial Chinese doctrine of the Five Phases, which categorizes everything in the universe according to five elements: wood, fire, earth, metal and water.

The idea of the "middle" is of special significance because it is reflected in the traditional name for China itself, *Zhongguo*. The word *guo* means "land", "kingdom" or "state", and can be translated as either plural or singular. So to Confucius (551–479BCE) and his contemporaries, *Zhongguo* meant the "Central States", the various kingdoms of the North China Plain whose collective territory defined the limits of Chinese civilization. Later, however, after the 221BCE unification under the First Emperor, the term *Zhongguo* came to be understood as a singular noun denoting the empire, the "Central State", or more poetically, the "Middle Kingdom". Throughout most of antiquity, *Zhongguo* was truly believed to be the centre of "all under Heaven", and surrounded on all (four) sides by barbarians.

At the centre of the empire itself was the emperor, represented by the extra fifth claw of his personal heraldic emblem, the imperial dragon (other Chinese dragons have just four claws, *see also* LONG DRAGON, *p48*). At the Forbidden City in Beijing, five bridges cross a symbolic canal, the middle bridge being reserved for the emperor alone. Today, the People's Republic has a flag with five stars; one is larger than the others, representing the Communist Party, the "centre" of modern Chinese society.

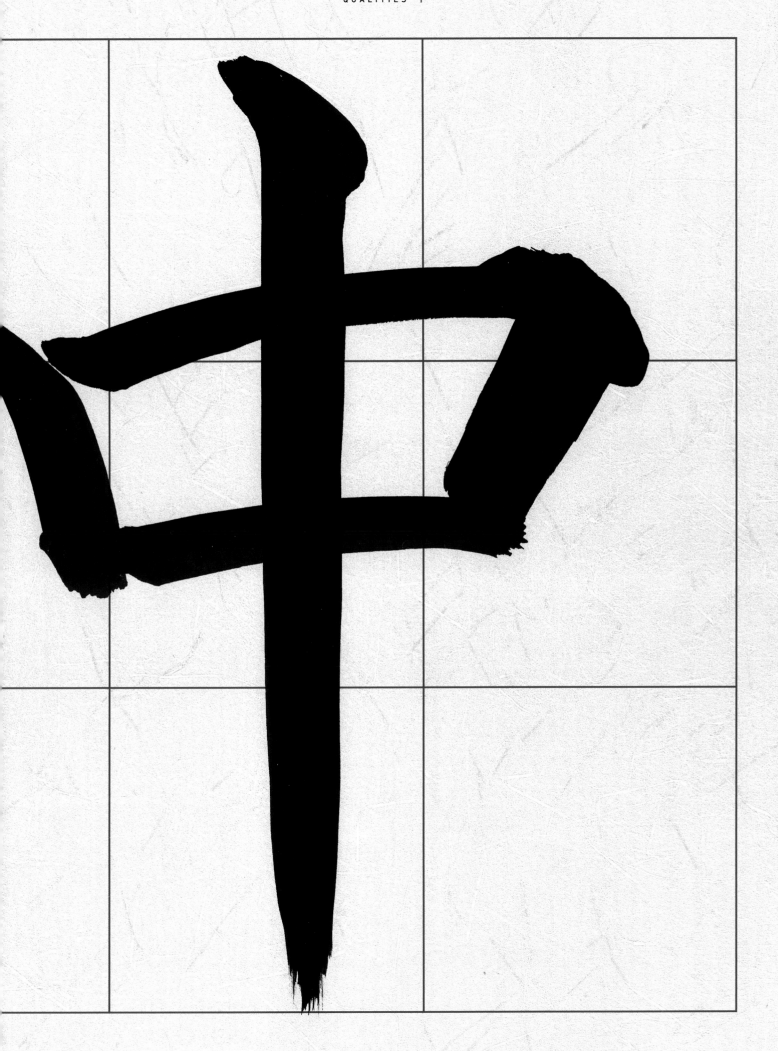

# LUCK

**FU**

福无双至，祸不单行

**"Blessings do not come in pairs, nor do misfortunes appear singly."**

Early forms of the character 福 *fu* appear to depict a wine vase or jar alongside a ritual tripod altar. The original idea was no doubt to convey the good fortune that, it was hoped, would follow from pleasing the gods and ancestors through the correct ritual offerings. One of the most auspicious of all characters, 福 *fu* means "luck", "happiness", "blessings" and "fulfilment".

Since at least the Song dynasty (960–1279), 福 *fu* has been one of the most frequently displayed characters in Chinese homes and businesses, especially at New Year. Often found by the entrance, the character is said to invite good fortune through the door and ward off poverty at the same time.

One common custom is to display the character upside down. *Dao* means "upside down" as well as "to come" in Chinese, and so *fu* displayed upside down conveys *fu dao*, meaning literally "*fu* upside down" but also "*fu* is coming". According to legend, this custom originated during the reign of the first Ming emperor, the brilliant and ruthless Hongwu (ruled 1368–1398). When passing through the capital with his troops, he saw that an illiterate family had pasted the character the wrong way up and, taking this as an act of insolence, ordered the family to be executed. But his consort the Empress Ma appeased him, and saved the innocent family, with the ingenious explanation that the family had known the emperor was due to pass and so had deliberately placed the character upside down to signify "a blessing is coming".

*Fu* can be depicted in art by a bat (also *fu*) and the hibiscus flower, known in Chinese as *furong*, which symbolizes happiness (*fu*) and honour (*rong*). The five cartoon mascots of the 2008 Beijing Olympics were called the *fuwa*, or "lucky children".

**LEFT:** *Flowers and Incense* (ca. 1720–1750), by Ding Liangxian. Probably given as a gift at Chinese New Year, this Qing dynasty woodblock print expresses wishes for peace, wealth, longevity, happiness and luck through a variety of symbols, including the bat (*fu*), which is a homophone of *fu* meaning "luck" or "happiness".

爱屋及乌
**"Love me, love my dog."**

# LOVE

**AI**

The earliest version of the character 愛 *ai*, meaning "love" or "affection", is made up of a radical that means "to breathe" or "to swallow" surrounding that for "heart", which in China as in many other cultures is traditionally thought to be the seat of love between human beings. To feel love toward something is therefore literally to swallow it into one's heart.

*Ai* is most commonly associated with a harmonious married life and a happy family. The love between husband and wife is frequently represented in Chinese art by a pair of mandarin ducks, because of

an old belief that these birds mate for life and will die if they are ever separated. According to one Han dynasty poem, two mandarin ducks once arose from the grave of two lovers, calling themselves the "birds of true love". Love is also symbolized by flowers such as bindweed (*Convolvulus*), red peonies – red being the colour of brides – and orchids. The character 愛 *ai* itself is considered an auspicious symbol, and is commonly used to decorate gifts or other tokens of affection.

For Buddhists, from China and elsewhere, the embodiment of love is the goddess Guanyin.

An immensely popular figure, Guanyin originated as a male bodhisattva – an enlightened being – named Avalokiteshvara in Sanskrit. His characteristics of love, mercy and compassion were considered primarily female virtues in China and by the 13th century depictions of this bodhisattva had become feminized, perhaps under the influence of native Chinese goddesses such as Xi Wang Mu (*see* WEST, *p167*).

In transliterating the names of foreign countries, Chinese language often employs syllables whose literal meanings are benevolent and auspicious.

Hence the word for "love" (*ai*) is used phonetically with those for "lattice" (*er*) and "orchid" (*lan*) – a flower traditionally associated with love – to give the name *Ai-er-lan* – Ireland.

有情人终成眷属

**"Passion can conquer anything to make a couple unite."**

# PASSION

**QING**

This complex character (情 *qing*) is what is known as a "phonetic compound". At the right is the radical for the homophone *qing*, meaning blue or green, to indicate the pronunciation. An abbreviated form of the character *xin*, meaning "heart", is at the left-hand side to indicate the meaning. *Xin* is also present in several other Chinese words that fall into the category "emotions".

*Qing* is almost impossible to translate with a single English word. In general it signifies human passion, feeling, sentiment or emotion, and the *qi qing* are the Seven Passions

– joy, anger, sorrow, fear, love, hatred and desire. *Qing* is also often used purely to denote love, synonymous with *ai* (*see opposite*). Thus, the word for "lover" is *qingren*, literally "passion person", and the Chinese equivalent of St Valentine's Day is *Qinrenjie* – "lovers' festival". In the preface to *Qing Shi* (*The History of Love*), which consists of 800 short tales about love, the Ming dynasty writer Feng Menglong (ca. 1574–1645) defined *qing* as the supreme principle governing human relationships.

However, as well as "passion" or "love", *qing* also means "facts",

"reality" or "circumstances", and the connection between the two seemingly distant areas of meaning has been much debated. The contemporary scholar Song Geng has called *qing* "a kind of sensibility to everything in the world, including not only human beings but also natural entities like the mountains, rivers, birds, grasses and so on." On the other hand, Confucianists claimed that when we perceive the harmonious reality (*qing*) of the natural world, we are inclined to benevolent and harmonious feelings (*qing*).

# LONGEVITY

**SHOU**

仁者寿

**"Those who have empathy for their fellow men enjoy a long life."**

The rather complex character 壽 *shou*, meaning "longevity", "long life" or "old age", combines two main elements. At the top is a radical that means "old", and beneath that a phonetic element *zhou*, meaning "to ask", which comprises a mouth below what, in the earliest extant form, was a wavy S-shaped figure. This lower element is a sort of "phonetic within a phonetic", because it in turn represented "ploughed fields" (also pronounced *zhou*).

The Chinese deeply respect the elderly, and they consider a long life – ideally accompanied by health and happiness – to be one of the most important blessings. The character 壽 *shou* therefore often appears on gifts and as a domestic decoration, and longevity is frequently represented in art by a wide range of motifs, such as pines, bamboo and plum blossoms (*see pp64, 66 and 72*), and, above all, peaches (*tao*). These fruits were associated with the powerful goddess Xi Wang Mu, the Queen Mother of the West (*see* WEST, *p167*), in whose gardens grew peaches that conferred the gift of immortal life and youth on the gods and goddesses. Depictions of the popular god of longevity Lao Shouxing are immediately recognizable by his enormous bulbous forehead, shaggy eyebrows and long earlobes. He almost invariably carries a large peach in one hand, and often a stick and a gourd containing life-prolonging elixirs in the other. This plump, elderly and gentle immortal is also commonly portrayed riding on a deer – another symbol of longevity (*see p56*).

Daoist alchemy – popular in China for centuries – was dedicated to prolonging, and indeed reversing altogether, the ageing process in pursuit of immortality. Gold, cinnabar (mercuric sulphide, the principal ore of mercury) and lead were among the ingredients of various elixirs prepared by Daoist alchemists such as the Jin dynasty official, Ge Hong (284–364CE) who particularly recommended the manufacture of *jin dan* ("gold elixir") as a means to achieve transcendence. Some of these elixirs had potentially lethal results, and in the Ming dynasty several emperors died quite young, at least partly as a result of following alchemist's recommendations.

**The many peaks of Mount Tianzi in Hunan province. Present on Earth since its creation, mountains are another important symbol of longevity in China. It was also believed that the finest minerals and herbs for making longevity elixirs could be found at their summit.**

# PEACE

**AN**

居安思危

**"Even in times of peace, one should be alert to possible danger."**

The earliest form of the character 安 an represents a woman inside a house, expressing a traditional ideal of peace, tranquillity, stability, safety and good order. In pre-modern China women rarely left the home, except in times of unrest or war, which may also contribute toward the association.

Peace is the essential condition for the harmonious functioning of society and the state, and has been a central concern in China since the time of Confucius, who vainly sought to persuade the various warring rulers of his day to absorb his precepts to bring about peace and social harmony. It was only several centuries later, when China was a united empire under the Han, that Chinese rulers finally adopted his theories as principles of government. These principles rested on the Confucian idea that Heaven (tian) granted the ruler a mandate to govern. It was the emperor's duty, therefore, to ensure that peace and harmony prevailed on Earth, as it did in the celestial realm of Heaven. If he failed to prevent unrest or war (as well as famine, plague and other natural disasters), he might forfeit the heavenly mandate and be legitimately overthrown. The great portal to the Forbidden City, the seat of China's last emperors, is called the Tiananmen, the gate (men) of heavenly peace.

Quails (also an) are often used to represent a message of peace in Chinese art. They will often be depicted in pairs, since shuang an means both a "pair of quails" and "may you [referring either to you and your spouse or to your parents] live in peace". Similarly, when there are nine of the birds, the message conveyed is jiu an, which signifies both "nine quails together" and "eternal peace", as does the combination of a quail (an) and a chrysanthemum (ju).

# FILIAL PIETY

**XIAO**

不孝有三，无后为大

*Mencius said,* "There are three ways of being unfilial, and the worst of them is to have no descendants."

The earliest form of the character 孝 *xiao*, meaning "filial piety", depicts a child supporting a figure that represents an aged parent (which in turn combines elements for "person", "hair" and "change" – literally, one whose hair changes).

According to Confucian morality, a stable and ordered society was constructed around certain key relationships, the most fundamental being that between parent and child. In Confucius's view, a child must demonstrate *xiao* – loving obedience and duty to their parents – and a parent in return owes their child loving and attentive care. This basic dynamic was echoed in several other relationships, such as that between husband and wife and between a ruler and his ministers. Complete equality in a relationship was supposed to be possible only between friends.

The *Twenty-Four Examples of Filial Piety* (*Er Shi Si Xiao*) was compiled by Guo Jujing in the Yuan dynasty, to encourage this essential Confucian virtue of reverence for parents. These widely known tales show the lengths to which exemplary individuals might go to please or care for their parents. In one famous tale, the 70-year-old Lao Laizi amuses his parents by acting like a child, dancing and turning somersaults. In another, Wang Xiang lies naked on a frozen river in order to melt a hole and catch a carp to cure the illness of his cruel stepmother, who at once repents of her harsh treatment of him.

The duties of filial piety extended to reverence for both ancestors and descendants. As the Confucian philosopher Mencius phrased it: "There are three ways of being unfilial, and the worst of them is to have no descendants." If this could not be done in the usual way, then families would often resort to adoption or, in the case of rich families, concubines.

# TRUST

**XIN**

美言不信

**"Beautiful language often cannot be trusted."**

A compound of the radicals for "person" and "word" or "speak" gives the original form of the character 信 *xin*, which means "trust", as well as other terms associated with a person being "as good as their word", such as "faith", "good faith", "fidelity", "confidence" and "truthfulness".

According to the *Analects*, compiled by Confucius's followers, "The Master taught four things: writings, ethics, loyalty, and *xin*". In the *Record of Ritual* (*Liji*), one of the Five Classics (*see* CLASSICS, *p146*), *xin* is described as one of the two fundamental prerequisites for the operation of a stable and just society, the other being peace (*see p176*). Elsewhere in the *Analects*, Confucius is also recorded as saying that governments require three things: sufficient food, sufficient military equipment, and the trust (*xin*) of the people. He goes on to say that for a ruler to hold on to power, the trust of the people is the least dispensable of these elements, for "if the people cease to trust their rulers, the state has no standing". Nor can a ruler govern effectively if he cannot trust his own ministers.

Confucius taught that much the same applies to personal relationships, which can only function when they are founded on trust. When asked how a man should behave in order to gain the respect of those around him, he replied: "Let his words be sincere and trustworthy (*xin*) and his actions be honourable and careful." Sincerity was what led to trust because, "if you are sincere, people will have faith (*xin*) in you." The philosopher Mozi (ca. 470–ca. 391BCE), who disagreed with many Confucian principles, defined *xin* more simply as "one's words agreeing with one's thoughts".

# LOYALTY

## ZHONG

忠孝不能两全

**"In a man's life, either loyalty to the emperor or filial piety to his parents has to be sacrificed."**

The character for loyalty (忠 *zhong*) is a compound of the radical for "middle" (*zhong*), an arrow hitting the centre of its target, as a pronunciation guide; and that for "heart", indicating that the word is connected to "emotions". The meanings of both elements together also strikingly convey the idea of faithful devotion – the heart that "hits the mark" or is "true".

Confucius is said to have taught four principal subjects, (*see opposite*), of which the most important were loyalty (*zhong*) and trust or good faith (*xin*). According to his pupil Zengzi (505–436BCE), *zhong* was "the one idea threading together" all his master's teachings. The Confucian doctrine of human relationships placed loyalty and faithfulness at the centre of the virtues that one must show to one's superiors, who would reciprocate by protecting and providing for those below them, according to the principles of filial piety (*see p178*). However, loyalty as defined in Confucian terms should not be a simple slavish obedience, since one also

has a duty to offer criticism to one's ruler or parent, if this will be of benefit. Loyalty should also be balanced by consideration for others (*shu*).

A popular decorative motif symbolizing loyalty, often found in workplaces, is the Eight Horses of King Mu (ruled ca. 976–ca. 922BCE). Mu was fond of travelling, and according to legend was borne around in a chariot pulled by eight horses – an auspicious number – each with its own special character and talent. Together the horses represent the fact that no matter how skilful they are, kings and commanders – and employers – will achieve little without the loyalty of those who serve them.

# BEAUTY

## MEI

英雄难过美人关

**"Even heroes can meet their downfall when tricked by beautiful women."**

The character 美 *mei* means "beauty" or "beautiful", and also "tasty" as well as, more generally, "nice". The earliest form of the character represents the horned head of a sheep or goat combined with the radical for "big", represented by a person with outstretched arms. For the majority of the ancient Chinese, who often struggled to avoid hunger, a fattened sheep or goat was no doubt a rare and special treat, and an apt way of representing something that was highly desirable. Another interpretation is that the animal head reflects an ancient belief that plumpness and a sheep-like gentleness and docility were markers of feminine beauty, as they were later under the Tang dynasty (618–907CE).

The word *mei* is a homophone of the Chinese word for "eyebrow" (*mei*), and traditionally eyebrows have been an important aspect of feminine beauty in China since at least the Han and Tang dynasties, when it was common for women to shave them off and then paint them back on in fashionable shapes (*see also* EYEBROW, *p84*). To this day an attractive young woman might find herself addressed as *mei mei*, "beautiful eyebrows".

*Mei* is also a homophone of *mei* meaning "plum blossom" (*see* PRUNUS, *p72*), whose five petals are emblems of the Five Happinesses (wealth, health, virtue, long life and peaceful death). One story recounts how a 5th-century princess named Shouyang was lying under a plum tree when a blossom landed on her forehead between her eyebrows, creating both an attractive imprint and a striking triple wordplay on the word *mei* – beauty, eyebrows and plum blossom. This started a fashion for appliqué forehead designs among the other ladies of court, beginning with paper plum blossoms but later, in the Tang dynasty, embracing a wide range of designs.

The word *mei* is also interestingly used in *Meiguo*, the Chinese rendering of "America" – literally "beautiful country".

**RIGHT: Watercolour of birds, fruit and plum blossom by Wang Guochen (late 19th century).**

富贵不归故乡，如衣锦夜行

**"If he does not return to his hometown when he becomes rich and famous, he is like one who wears beautiful clothes and stays in the dark."**

# PRESTIGE

**GUI**

An image of hands presenting a vessel makes up the oldest form of the character 貴 *gui*, meaning "prestige", "esteem", "honour" (also in the sense of an accolade) and "high rank", and related senses such as "esteemed" and "noble" as well as "prized" and "precious". *Gui* plus the word *zu* (meaning "clan" or "family") gives *gui zu*, meaning both "aristocracy" and "nobleman" or "noblewoman".

Prestige or honour is highly desirable in China, but traditionally can only be earned through ethical conduct. As Confucius said, "All men long for wealth and prestige. But if they cannot acquire them in the correct manner, they should not receive them." For him, riches and honours "gained by unrighteousness" were as insubstantial "as a floating cloud". Similarly, honours were worthless and even "shameful" if they derived from a bad ruler.

*Gui* was marked and respected in daily life in dynastic China. In the Tang dynasty, senior government officials of Grade Three and above would have a ceremonial halberd (an axe-blade attached to a pole) outside their residence, to convey their prestige. If a family was lucky enough to have three members of this rank, then there would be three halberds, and the title "three-halberd" would be incorporated into their family name, to display their influence and place in society. Later on, the phrase "three halberds" on its own became an allusion to prestige.

In Chinese art, *gui* may be symbolized by the homophonous sweet olive tree (*see p74*), which is also *gui*. Combined with peaches, a traditional emblem of longevity (*see p174*), osmanthus conveys a wish for long life and high rank. A depiction of osmanthus alongside seeds or nuts, which represent (male) children, expresses a hope for "precious sons" and also "sons who will reach high rank". One 15th-century carpenter's manual recommended placing a leaf of osmanthus in the bracket of a wooden pillar as a talisman to assist the sons of the house to pass the imperial examinations and go on to achieve senior rank (*gui*) in the civil service.

**RIGHT: Silk badge of rank from a Qing dynasty court official's robe, featuring an embroidered dragon (19th century).**

# CHRONOLOGY OF DYNASTIES AND NOTABLE EMPERORS

### PREHISTORIC PERIOD
**Xia dynasty (ca. 2050–ca. 1500BCE)**
*A semi-legendary dynasty probably connected with the culture based at the late Neolithic site of Erlitou in Henan province.*

### HISTORIC PERIOD
**Shang dynasty (ca. 1500–ca. 1050BCE)**

**Zhou dynasty (ca. 1046–221BCE)**

*Western Zhou (ca. 1046–770BCE)*

*Eastern Zhou (ca. 770–221BCE)*

*Spring and Autumn Period (770–481BCE)*
In this period the Zhou succession continued, but China was divided into *de facto* independent states, mostly ruled by dukes (*gong*) or marquises (*hou*), nominally loyal to the Zhou. The rulers of the state of Chu assumed the title of king (*wang*).

*Warring States Period (453–221BCE)*
In this period the rulers of several states, including Qin, also took the title *wang*.

### IMPERIAL PERIOD
**Qin dynasty (221–207BCE)**
Qin Shi Huangdi (The First Emperor 221–210BCE).

**Han dynasty (206BCE–220CE)**
*Western Han (206BCE–8CE)*
Gaozu (206–195BCE)
Wu Di (141–87BCE)
Wang Mang ("Xin dynasty" interregnum, 9–25CE)

*Eastern Han (25–220CE)*
Guangwu Di (25–57)
Ming Di (57–76)
He Di (88–106)
Xian Di (190–220)

### PERIOD OF DISUNION
**Three Kingdoms (220–265)**

*Wei (220–264)* Rulers of north China
*Shu Han (221–263)* Rulers of west China
*Wu (222–280)* Rulers of east China

**Western Jin dynasty (265–316)**
*Wu (265–290)*

**Northern and Southern dynasties (317–581)**

*Northern dynasties*
Northern (Tuoba) Wei (386–534)
Western Wei (534–557)
Eastern Wei (534–550)
Northern Qi (550–577)
Northern Zhou (557–581)

*Southern dynasties*
Eastern Jin (317–420)
Liu Song (420–479)
Southern Qi (479–502)
Liang (502–557)
Chen (557–589)

### ERA OF THE TANG
**Sui dynasty 581–618**
Wen Di (581–604)
Yang Di (604–618)

**Tang dynasty 618–907**
Gaozu (618–626)
Taizong (626–649)
Gaozong (649–684)
Ruizong (684–690, 710–712)
Wu Zetian ("Zhou Dynasty" interregnum, 690–705). *China's only female emperor.*
Xuanzong (712–756)

### FIVE DYNASTIES & TEN KINGDOMS
**Five Dynasties (ruled in the north, 907–960)**

**Ten Kingdoms (ruled in the south, 907–960)**

### AGE OF THE SONG
**Song dynasty (960–1279)**
*Northern Song (960–1126)*
Taizu (960–976)
Taizong (976–997)
Huizong (1101–1125)

**Southern Song (1127–1279)**
Gaozong (1127–1162)

**Liao (Khitan) dynasty 907–1119**

**Jin (Jurchen) dynasty 1115–1234**

### AGE OF AUTOCRACY
**Yuan (Mongol) dynasty 1279–1368**
Khubilai Khan (Yuan Shizu, 1279–1294)

**Ming dynasty 1368–1644**
Hongwu (1368–1398)
Yongle (1402–1424)

**Qing dynasty 1644–1911**
Shunzhi (1644–1662)
Kangxi (1662–1722)
Yongzheng (1722–1736)
Qianlong (1736–1796)
Guangxu (1875–1908). *Dowager Empress Cixi (1835–1908) was de facto ruler for most of the reign.*
Xuantong (Puyi, 1909–1911)

### NOTE ON EMPERORS' TITLES
*Chinese emperors from the Han to the end of the Yuan are known by their "temple names" – posthumous titles by which they were venerated in ancestral rites. Temple names often include the syllables zu and zong, meaning "ancestor" or "founder". Hence, Liu Bang, the founder of the Han, and Li Yuan, the founder of the Tang, are both known by the temple name Gaozu ("exalted founder" or "ancestor"). Ming and Qing emperors are known by their "era names". Emperors commonly divided their reigns into eras with auspicious names, a practice still followed in Japan. A ruler might adopt several era names during his reign, but Ming and Qing emperors used only one era name to cover the whole reign. Thus, the Ming emperor Chengzu named his reign Yongle (Perpetual Happiness), so he is referred to as the "Yongle emperor", which is often used as if it were a personal name, the "Emperor Yongle". The three famous emperors of the Qing are now often called Kangxi, Yongzheng and Qianlong rather than "the Kangxi emperor," and so on.*

# BIBLIOGRAPHY

Chiang Yee, *Chinese Calligraphy*. Methuen: London, 1961.

Chinnery, John, *Treasures of China*. Duncan Baird Publishers: London, 2008.

Eberhard, Wolfram, trans. by G.L. Campbell, *A Dictionary of Chinese Symbols*. Routledge: London and New York, 1986.

Ecke, Tseng Yu-ho, *Chinese Calligraphy*. Philadelphia Museum of Art: Philadelphia, 1971.

Fazzioli, Edoardo, *Chinese Calligraphy: From Pictograph to Ideogram*. Abbeville Press: New York and London, 1987.

Lindqvist, Cecilia, trans. by Joan Tate, *China: Empire of Living Symbols*. Addison-Wesley: New York, 1989.

Norman, Jerry, *Chinese*. Cambridge University Press: Cambridge,1988.

Shaughnessy, Edward L. (General Editor), *China*. Duncan Baird Publishers: London, 2000.

Song Geng, *The Fragile Scholar: Power and Masculinity in Chinese Culture*. Hong Kong University Press: Hong Kong, 2004.

Bjaaland Welch, Patricia, *Chinese Art: A Guide to Motifs and Visual Imagery*. Tuttle Publishing: Singapore, 2008.

Williams, C.A.S., *Chinese Symbolism and Art Motifs*. Tuttle Publishing: Singapore 1974.

**BOOKS IN CHINESE**

*7000 han zi wu ti mao bi shu fa zi dian* (*A Dictionary of 7000 Chinese Characters in Five Calligraphic Scripts*). Zhejiang Ancient Books Publishing House: Hangzhou, 2005.

*Han yu da ci dian* (*The Grand Dictionary of Chinese Characters*). Hubei Dictionary Publishing House and Sichuan Dictionary Publishing House: Hubei and Sichuan, 1995.

Zuo Min'an, *Xi shuo han zi* (*A Detailed Account of 1000 Chinese Characters*). Jiuzhou Press: Beijing, 2005.

# CHARACTER INDEX

# INDEX

References to picture captions are in **bold**,
references to character entries are in *italics*

# ACKNOWLEDGMENTS AND PICTURE CREDITS

## AUTHOR'S ACKNOWLEDGMENTS

I feel privileged to have been entrusted with this project by Duncan Baird Publishers, and am grateful to my editor Kirty Topiwala for acting as my instructor and steering me clear of many obstacles during the course of the book's completion. Many thanks also to Peter Bently for his research and support in writing the character entries.

## PICTURE CREDITS

The publisher would like to thank the following people, museums and photographic libraries for permission to reproduce their material. Every care has been taken to trace copyright holders. However, if we have omitted anyone we apologize and will, if informed, make corrections to any future edition.

T = top
B = bottom
L = left
R = right

**Front & Back Endpapers:** Collector's colophon of *The Admonitions Scroll* © The Trustees of the British Museum, London; **page 4** Deng Shiru, *Poem on seeing off Adjutant Administrator Zhu*, hanging scroll © Freer Gallery of Art, Smithsonian Institution, Washington D.C. Purchase – Regents' Collections Acquisition Program, (F1980.5); **6** © RMN / Ravaux / Musée Guimet, Paris; **11** © RMN / Thierry Ollivier / Musée Guimet, Paris **12** © The Trustees of the British Museum, London; **13 T** © Freer Gallery of Art, Smithsonian Institution, Washington D.C. Purchase – E. Rhodes and Leona B. Carpenter Foundation in honour of the 75th Anniversary of the Freer Gallery of Art (F1998.37); **13 B** Werner Forman Archive, London / National Palace Museum, Taipei; **14–15** © Freer Gallery of Art, Smithsonian Institution, Washington D.C. Gift of Peggy and Richard M. Danziger in honour of Pauline and Johnny Falk, (F1997.26); **17 L** Getty Images / AFP / HOANG DINH NAM; **17 R** Getty Images / Altrendo; **22–23** Getty Images / Peter Adams; **30** © RMN / Ghislain Vanneste / Musée Guimet, Paris; **31** Christie's Images Ltd, London; **36** Getty images / joSon; **38–39** Corbis / JAI / Michele Falzone; **48** © The Palace Museum, Beijing; **50–51** Bridgeman Art Library / Museum of Fine Arts, Boston, Massachusetts / Francis Gardner Curtis Fund; **54** © RMN / Jean-Gilles Berizzi / Musée Guimet, Paris; **59** © RMN / Ghislain Vanneste / Musée Guimet, Paris; **64–65** Getty Images / The Image Bank / Jeff Hunter; **66–67** Bridgeman Art Library / FuZhai Archive; **70–71** Bridgeman Art Library / Osaka Museum of Fine Arts, Japan; **72** Christie's Images Ltd, London; **81** © The Trustees of the British Museum, London; **86** © V&A Images,Victoria and Albert Museum, London; **93** Bridgeman Art Library / Museum of Fine Arts, Boston, Massachusetts / Denman Waldo Ross Collection; **94** Bridgeman Art Library / Bibliothèque Nationale de France, Paris; **96** Photolibrary.com / Erwin Nielsen; **102–103** Art Archive, London / Private Collection; **107** Christie's Images Ltd, London; **110–111** Photolibrary.com / age Fotostock / Doco Dalfiano; **116** Photolibrary.com / Imagestate / Steve Vidler; **126–127** Getty Images / Stone / Michael McQueen; **131** Bridgeman Art Library / Archives Charmet / Private Collection; **132** Werner Forman Archive, London / Private Collection; **135** Scala, Florence / Art Resource / Image © The Metropolitan Museum of Art. Purchase, Friends of Asian Art Gifts, 1987 (1987.147); **139** © V&A Images, Victoria and Albert Museum, London; **142–143** Plainpicture / T Rüggeberg; **155** Bridgeman Art Library / Paul Freeman / Private Collection; **162** © V&A Images, Victoria and Albert Museum, London; **163** Photolibrary.com / Nancy Brown; **170** © The Trustees of the British Museum, London; **174–175** Getty Images / The Image Bank / Peter Adams; **176** Werner Forman Archive, London / Stein Collection, British Museum, London; **183** Bridgeman Art Library / School of Oriental & African Studies Library, University of London; **185** Werner Forman Archive, London / Private Collection.